MAN IN HIS RIGHT MIND

THIS BOOK PROVIDES an integration of psychology and Christian belief which is long overdue. It is a thoroughly reliable and helpful attempt to remove barriers of thought which have grown up, and to relate what is true in the leading psychological schools to what the Christian already accepts on Biblical grounds. It dispels two false suppositions – that psychologists are "desecrators of holy ground", and that psychiatry has disproved Christianity, explained away God, conversion, and the significance of guilt, and virtually regards man as little more than a complex bundle of reflexes.

The author has made a deep study of the writers he discusses and their schools of thought, and has expounded their views in ways that can be grasped by the intelligent, non-specialist reader. But he refuses to keep his knowledge as a psychologist in a separate compartment from his beliefs as an avowed Christian, and in this book he shows that Christian belief goes beyond the more immediate goal of neutral psychology and psychiatry, and is, according to the New Testament pattern, "man in his right mind" – a being spiritually and psychologically in harmony, right with himself and his fellow-man because he is first right with God.

INTERNATIONAL CHRISTIAN
GRADUATE UNIVERSITY

TITLES IN THIS SERIES

MAN
IN HIS
RIGHT MIND

Harold W. Darling, M.A. Ph.D.

Professor of Psychology, Spring Arbor College, Michigan

With a Preface by
CANON J. STAFFORD WRIGHT, M.A.

the *Attic Press*, Inc.
GREENWOOD, S. C.

ISBN: 0 85364 097 1

AUSTRALIA:

Emu Book Agencies Ltd.,
63 Berry St., Granville 2142, N.S.W.

SOUTH AFRICA:
Oxford University Press,
P.O. Box 1141, Cape Town

*Cover photograph by courtesy of Specialised Laboratory
Equipment, Campbell Road, Croydon, and Laurence
Evans*

*Made and Printed in Great Britain
by Butler & Tanner Ltd, Frome and London*

TO

OLLIE, BARBARA AND TERRY

Contents

Preface

by CANON J. STAFFORD WRIGHT, M.A.

CHRISTIANS ARE OFTEN as uneasy in the presence of psychology as psychologists and psychiatrists are in the presence of Christianity. If psychologists seem to desecrate "holy ground", Christians in their turn are thought to be the cause and support of some of the twists that bring people for treatment. Meanwhile the casual onlooker supposes that psychology has disproved Christianity, explained away God, conversion, and the significance of guilt, and in some cases turned man into little more than a complex bundle of reflexes.

This division is a tragedy. Whatever truth has been discovered about the structure and development of human beings – not to mention other animals! – cannot contradict any other truth, and certainly not the revealed truth that Christians accept. Hypotheses to explain certain factors in mankind, both collectively and as individuals, certainly differ from School to School. There is no agreed psychological map of man, and the Christian who wants to understand himself will need to sift assured or probable truth from emotional deductions that he and others may want to draw.

This book is a thoroughly helpful attempt to break down barriers, and to relate what is true in the leading psychological Schools to what the Christian accepts on Biblical grounds. The author has made a deep study of the writers he discusses, and has expounded their views in ways that can be grasped intelligently; but he refuses to keep his knowledge as a psychologist in a separate compartment from his beliefs as a Christian. To him truth is one, and this is as it should be.

While personal faith should not cloud one's presentation of truth, some writers are over-cautious in involving themselves. As an example, on page 104 Dr. Darling writes of Jung's God as "simply the God-image within us." This is a true judgement of Jung's writings as an investigating psychologist. But, writing privately of his personal belief, Jung said, "How on earth did you get the idea that I could replace God – and with a concept at that? I can establish the existence of psychological wholeness to which our consciousness is subordinate and which is, in itself, beyond precise description. But this 'self' can never take the place of God, although it may, perhaps, be a receptacle for divine grace." (Quoted by Victor White, *God and the Unconscious*, p. 248).

There is no such misunderstanding of Dr. Darling's position. He is an avowed Christian, and in this book he shows that the Christian goal, according to the New Testament pattern, is man in his right mind. This Christian goal takes us beyond the goal of neutral psychology and psychiatry, but it is backed by what psychologists have found experimentally in their researches into the inner world and outer responses of men, women, and children.

MAN IN HIS RIGHT MIND

I

The Nature of Man

EVER SINCE PSYCHOLOGY became a separate science, with the establishment of its first laboratory by Wilhelm Wundt in 1879 — and even long before that — great thinkers have been asking, "What is man?" Personality, mind, soul, motivation, will, conscience, guilt and many other dimensions of our being have long intrigued philosophers, scientists, theologians and psychologists. We have, it would seem, an insatiable capacity for self-study and introspection, with the result that the literature is replete with more or less systematic attempts to explain our nature.

The common "religion" of our day places man at its center, a fact that is causing great concern to many present-day thinkers. Theologians maintain that to find our highest degree of self-fulfillment, we must relate ourselves properly to God, and in such a relationship find meaning in this present life as well as the assurance of bliss in the life to come. Psychologists, while generally reasoning from non-theological suppositions, have frequently arrived at a rather similar conclusion: if we are to find meaning and direction in the here and now, if we are to reach the highest levels of adjustment, we must find a cause greater than ourselves around which to integrate.

Prior to the impact of psychology, Darwinianism, and humanism our insights about ourselves were typically

achieved within a religious perspective. More recently, however, our self-study takes on but two dimensions: we look
introspectively at ourselves and objectively at others. In
other words, our present tendency is to look both inward
and outward, rather than upward.

An accurate, insightful look into our true nature is an
appropriate and essential first stage in a book dealing with
moral issues in psychology. In this first chapter concepts
relating to our nature are divided into five categories: we
are viewed as inherently moral, immoral and amoral, as
existential beings, and, finally, in Christian perspective.

Man Is Good

The thrust of the humanistic philosophers from the eigh-
teenth century to the present, as well as such notables before
them as Confucius and Mencius, has been that our inherent
humanity leads us to increasingly higher stages of development. We carry within us not only our individuality but
also the potentialities of all humanity. The task of life, then,
is to develop toward totality through individuality.[1]

Rousseau, the great champion of humanism, declares that
all of the gifts from the hands of the "Author of Nature"
are good. The first impulses of nature are invariably right;
there is no original sin in the human heart; the hows and
whys of every vice are traceable.[2]

Erich Fromm's point of view is rather typical of humanistic thought: as normal persons we carry within ourselves a
tendency toward development and productivity; to lack these
is to possess symptoms of mental illness. While the incentive
for mental health is universal, environmental forces operating against us may, and frequently do, interfere with this
incentive.[3] Provided with a good growing ground, specific-

---

[1]Erich Fromm, *Beyond the Chains of Illusion* (New York: Simon
and Schuster, 1962), pp. 28-29.

[2]Stella Van Petten Henderson, *Introduction to Philosophy of Education* (Chicago: The University of Chicago Press, 1947), p. 30.

[3]Erich Fromm, *Man for Himself* (New York: Rinehart and Company, 1947), pp. 218-19.

ally a good education and positive environmental influences and experiences, we may be expected to mature naturally into a state of personal and social well-being and usefulness. We have little or no need for Divine help; we are capable of working out our own salvation. That we have rarely reached this high ideal is summarily explained away as the fault of the corrupting influences of society.

A number of modern-day psychologists have been strong adherents of this philosophy. Among them is Carl Rogers, who avows that the innermost core of our nature is basically socialized, positive, forward-moving, constructive and trustworthy.[4] We are self-actualizing creatures, experiencing the same biological unfolding that is characteristic of all living things.[5] All of the sensory and visceral experiences are organized into one system that is consistent with and related to the self.[6]

Similarly, A. H. Maslow contends that the organism is more trustworthy, self-protecting and self-governing than we usually give it credit for being. Our thrust is toward growth and self-actualization.[7] Our inborn nature is essentially good and is never evil. When we are sinful, unhappy or neurotic, it is our environment that makes us that way. While environment may well play a supportive role in our self-actualization, it is enough that environment 'stand aside' and not interfere with our development.[8] Maslow's confidence in our positive and healthy qualities has led him to postulate a psychological "Eupsychia"[9] which might well evolve if a thousand of our healthiest families were to migrate

[4]Carl R. Rogers, *On Becoming a Person* (Boston: Houghton Mifflin Company, 1961), pp. 91, 194.

[5]Magda B. Arnold and John A. Gasson, *The Human Person* (New York: The Ronald Press, 1954), p. 179.

[6]Carl R. Rogers, *Client-Centered Therapy* (Boston: Houghton Mifflin Company, 1951), pp. 513-14.

[7]Abraham H. Maslow, *Motivation and Personality* (New York: Harper and Brothers, 1954), p. 124.

[8]Calvin S. Hall and Gardner Lindzey, *Theories of Personality* (New York: John Wiley and Sons, 1957), p. 326.

[9]Maslow, *Motivation and Personality*, p. 350.

to a deserted area where they could work out their destiny as they please.

Man Is Evil

In contrast to Rousseau, Rogers and Maslow, traditional theology has laid heavy emphasis upon the doctrine of inherent depravity. Drawing support from the Scriptures, theologians and Christian leaders past and present have contended for the truth of this doctrine. A perfect creation originally, Adam nevertheless sinned, so that the cry of King David, "Behold, I was brought forth in iniquity, and in sin did my mother conceive me," (Psalm 51:5)[10] speaks of the spiritual condition of all of us.

Augustine reasons that Adam's sin of disobedience set up an endless train of psychic inheritance, and that every child born since suffers the curse of a depraved nature. Only by Divine intervention can we be saved from this universally inherited tendency. Such a position emphasizes submission and dependence, condemns us to a psychological hopelessness, and declares us incapable of working out our own psychological salvation. Instead of being encouraged to develop all of our human powers and overcome obstacles, we have been taught to distrust and malign ourselves, and remain as dependent children. Our childhood temper tantrums have been viewed as evidences of evil will, and our stubbornness and disobedience are "badnesses" needing to be exorcised as if they were from Satan himself.[11]

Our depravity leaves us no freedom to choose the right. Martin Luther, assuming the existence of the innate viciousness and evil in our nature which directs our will toward evil, concludes[12] that it is impossible for us to perform any good deed on the basis of our nature.

---

[10]Note: Biblical references, unless otherwise indicated, are from the Revised Standard Version.

[11]Harry A. Overstreet, *The Mature Mind* (New York: W. W. Norton and Company, 1949), pp. 261-63.

[12]Erich Fromm, *Escape from Freedom* (New York: Holt, Rinehart and Winston, 1941), p. 74.

Gordon Clark maintains[13] that the most unmistakable of all truths is the deep-seated savagery and inherent evil in the human heart. Civilization and education may put a veneer over our nature that lasts for a time, but before long we "show our true colors."

Theologians continue to give assent to this view of human nature. Reinhold Niebuhr, e.g., describes our condition as essentially self-centered, so that we continually seek aggrandizement of self and domination over others. While this tendency may be checked to a large degree within the interdependent family, it is compounded in the larger society.[14]

Harvey Cox postulates[15] that all of us are sinners who suffer from a deformed and distorted vision of ourselves, society and reality in general. The Scriptures describe this condition with a wealth of similes that add evidence to the concept that we are sinful; we are variously labelled as lame, deaf, asleep, blind, dead, bewitched, in a stupor, in chains, in darkness and in prison.

While psychoanalysis and conservative theology have little in common, they are agreed that the nature of man is evil. Freud's basic concept of man is a most negative one. We are in essential conflict between the demands of our super-ego, or conscience, and the pressures of our unconscious repository of aggressive and sexual impulses, or id. Caught between, we have little alternative but to suffer by either denying ourselves the satisfaction of our instinctual drives, or to give vent to these cravings and thus be forced to suffer society's penalty for failure to live within its mores. The results are, at best, an inevitable hostility toward frustrating objects that serve to deny erotic satisfaction, or, at worst, the destruction of our lives as well as our civilization through flagrant gratification of these desires.

---

[13]Gordon H. Clark, *A Christian Philosophy of Education* (Grand Rapids: Eerdmans, 1946), p. 60.

[14]Frank N. Magill, ed., *Masterpieces of World Philosophy in Summary Form* (New York: Harper and Brothers, 1961), p. xxii.

[15]Harvey Cox, *The Secular City* (New York: The Macmillan Company, 1965), p. 118.

Freud views us[16] as machines driven by relatively constant
amounts of sexual energy, called libido, causing painful tension that can be eliminated only by acts of physical release.
To this liberation he gives the name pleasure. After a reduction of tension, libido increases again, causing a new need
for tension reduction, or pleasurable satisfaction. This dyna-
mism, which leads us from tension to release to more tension (or from pain to pleasure to pain), is the pleasure
principle. This principle contrasts or conflicts with the
reality principle which tells us what to seek for and what
to avoid in our world in order to survive.

Adherents of the depravity principle draw support for their
position through observation of the young child. Edward
Ames,[17] e.g., suggests that it is customary to regard children
as outside the social order, as at least aliens and perhaps even
enemies to the interests which adults consider vital. Our im-
pulsive, unreflective nature as children puts us frequently in
opposition to the established order of society and makes us appear rebellious and lacking in reverence. No wonder theologians regard us as sinful and perverse by nature, without
the capacity for any good thought or deed, until miraculously
regenerated by the power of God!

While it may be that as young children we begin life innocently enough, Boggs[18] observes, somehow in the good and
necessary act of discovering our freedom we come to the
inevitable self-assertive and rebellious use of will. This does
not occur all at once in a particular act, for different types of
rebellion characterize different age levels. It comes as the
repetitious "no" of the toddler; as the subtle and self-conscious
resistance to parental instructions by the eleven-year-old; as
the important, and even life-determining crises of adoles-

---

[16]Fromm, *Beyond the Chains of Illusion*, pp. 31-32.
[17]Edward Scribner Ames, "Religion and Childhood," in *Readings
in the Psychology of Religion*, ed. by Orlo Strunk, Jr. (New York:
Abingdon Press, 1959), p. 154.
[18]Wade H. Boggs, Jr., *All Ye Who Labor* (Richmond: John Knox
Press, 1961), pp. 117-18.

cence; and in due time as the overwhelming competitions and conflicts for self-advantage in adulthood.

MAN IS NEITHER GOOD NOR EVIL

Charles Darwin's theory of evolution has provided a powerful counteracting force to the concept of inherent depravity. Evolutionists contend that as long as we consider ourselves to be creatures apart from the rest of the living world, as "fallen angels" rather than as products of nature, we fail even to begin to understand ourselves.[19]

Many modern writers object to morality (that is, either goodness or badness) becoming the theoretical framework for our discussion of the nature of man. Overstreet[20] maintains that the goodness-badness theory is thoroughly misleading, and that a maturity-immaturity viewpoint is a much more appropriate evaluation of the human situation. We are not evil; we simply have grown to adult stature without becoming mature mentally, socially or emotionally. Human misbehaviors (sins) are simply immature ways of solving problems that ideally should be solved maturely. Counseling and mental hygiene clinics are proof, he claims, that this theory has "arrived." When Christ cried, "Forgive them; for they know not what they do," He looked upon His tormentors not as bad, but rather as too immature to recognize that their cruelty was cruelty.

The amoral point of view is traceable at least back to the philosopher, John Locke, who maintains that we are at birth a blank page (*tabula raza*), and that all the sensations, impressions and experiences of life implant themselves upon our impressionable brains. Contemporary American psychologists who subscribe to associationism in any of its forms, consider us likewise to be blank sheets of paper upon which our culture writes its text. We are viewed essentially as products of stimulus-response bonds, with no power of choice and with little ability to control our environment. To behavior-

---

[19]Henderson, *Introduction to Philosophy*, p. 20.
[20]Overstreet, *The Mature Mind*, p. 93.

ists, mind, soul, consciousness and purpose are superfluous abstractions and unrealities.[21]

MAN IS AN EXISTENTIAL BEING

Existential Philosophy

The philosophical movement called existentialism represents a radical departure from the objectivistic and mechanistic viewpoints of man. Christian existentialists, such as Kierkegaard and Marcel, as well as atheistic existentialists like Heidegger and Sartre, appear to have one common belief (and perhaps only one) — namely, that existence precedes essence. Existence is the awareness of the unity of the past, present and future, or that which we experience; while essence is the sensing of the object, or the distinctive nature of something.[22]

What makes us persons, deBeauvoir suggests, is our refusal to be passive, an urge that thrusts us toward things with the aim of dominating and shaping them.[23] Sartre[24] describes us as nothing else but what we make of ourselves. This is the first principle of existentialism. We are nothing else than our plan, than the ensemble of life's acts; we exist only to the extent that we fulfill ourselves.

Heidegger[25] sees us as possessing three fundamental features: factuality — we are already involved in the world; existentialism — we are projects and possibilities which have been but also which can become; and fallenness — we have the tendency to become mere presences in the world, failing to make the most of our possibilities. Through resolution, however, we move in time from the past to the future through the present, appraising ourselves, choosing with the

---

[21]Henderson, *Introduction to Philosophy*, p. 202.

[22]Magill, ed., *Masterpieces*, p. xxii.

[23]Simone deBeauvoir, "An Existentialist Looks at Americans," *New York Times Magazine*, May 25, 1947, p. 13.

[24]Ralph B. Winn, *A Concise Dictionary of Existentialism* (New York: Philosophical Library, 1960), pp. 63-64.

[25]Magill, *Masterpieces*, p. 886.

whole of our being and thereby achieving authentic existence.

Existential Psychology

Existential psychology, pioneered by Kierkegaard and perpetuated by Sartre, is a force within existentialism that speaks forcefully to our human condition. Among others, Viktor Frankl and Rollo May have made significant contributions to existentialist psychology. They have traversed beyond the pessimism and unconvincing freedom that existentialists generally give us.

Frankl's logotherapy, sometimes referred to as the Third Viennese School of Psychotherapy, is built upon the tenets of the other two schools of Vienna, Freud's Psychoanalysis and Adler's Individual Psychology. The aim of logotherapy[26] is not to supplant the other schools, but to complement them, picturing personality in a wholeness that includes the spiritual aspect.

We are three-dimensional beings: physical, psychological and spiritual. We have a body and we have a psyche (a system of innate drives), but we *are* a spiritual being.[27] The essence of this spiritual dimension is the will-to-meaning. Animals may engage in behavior which is purposeful, but it is never meaningful.

Our main concern in life is for meaning, which materializes through the actualization of three types of values: creative, experiential and attitudinal.[28] Creative values and experiential values give a meaning to human life that is judged by the peaks reached in moments of intense experiencing. Attitudinal values can be realized when there are no creative or experiential opportunities available (e.g., during intense suffering), and

---

[26]Viktor E. Frankl, *The Doctor and the Soul,* trans. by Richard and Clara Winston. (2nd edition; New York: Alfred A. Knopf, 1966), p. xii.

[27]Donald F. Tweedie, Jr., *Logotherapy and the Christian Faith* (Grand Rapids: Baker Book House, 1965), p. 56.

[28]See pp. 114-15 of this book for further elaboration of these values.

are measured by our specific reactions of courage and patience under the most adverse conditions.[29] "He who has a *why* to live for," Nietzsche affirms, and Frankl re-affirms, "can bear with almost any *how*."[30]

Frankl's view of our human condition is far from armchair theorizing or textbook eclecticism, but is the product of many years of clinical experience, during which time he has worked with thousands of patients in a psychiatric clinic and prisoners in a concentration camp. In his philosophy, the dignity of man remains central.

Three closely related factors characterize human existence: our spirituality, freedom and responsibility. We have freedom in spite of our instincts, inheritance and environment, and it is this freedom that distinguishes us from animals. Faced with life and conscious of our responsibility toward it, we have an obligation to carry out the life task imposed upon us. We are not to ask what we expect from life, but, rather, what life expects from us.[31] We must shoulder our own responsibility and fulfill our obligation if our lives are to be wholesome and meaningful. We are encouraged to do so by remembering to live as if we were living the *second time* and had acted as wrongly the first time as we are about to act now.[32]

We are more than the products of our heredity and environment; we ultimately decide for ourselves. Our freedom is not so much a freedom *from* as a freedom *for* something, and even a freedom *before somebody*. Our responsibility is to our conscience and, ultimately, to God. The only plausible ground for the conscience, for Frankl, is God, the Transcendent Being.[33] We are His Creation, made in His own image. We have the potentialities to be swine or saints within ourselves; which one is actualized depends on decisions, not on condi-

---

[29]Arnold and Gasson, *The Human Person*, p. 466.

[30]Viktor E. Frankl, *Man's Search for Meaning*, trans. by Ilse Lasch. (Revised edition; Boston: Beacon Press, 1962), p. 76.

[31]Frankl, *The Doctor*, pp. xi, xix.

[32]Arnold and Gasson, *The Human Person*, p. 468.

[33]Tweedie, *Logotherapy*, pp. 33, 62.

tions.[34] While the id and the superego can make demands, the self decides whether to grant or to refuse them.[35]

Rollo May's views on the nature of man are somewhat similar to Frankl's. While there are, unquestionably, compelling forces that impinge upon our personalities, we nevertheless have a margin of freedom. Both of these men rebel against the pervasive tendency to view ourselves as the willy-nilly products of the powerful Juggernaut of forces within and without. If we can become aware of that element of freedom, we are aided toward the realization of the element of decision at any given moment.[36] We have the ability, which is a characteristic of our existence, to transcend our immediate situation. In the constant process of becoming, we may transcend our past and present by reaching for the future.[37]

As persons, we are endowed with four salient characteristics: freedom, individuality, social integration and religious tension. Reacting against the Freudian concept of determinism, May insists on the freedom of human personality. Healthy persons are able to hold various impulses in "undecided balance," before finally making the decision whereby one prevails.[38]

May sanctions Sartre's contention that freedom is the central and unique potentiality that constitutes man as a human being. Freedom, to May, is a quality of the centered self. It is not the will controlling the mind, nor an autonomy of the self over the unconscious or over the body. We earn our freedom and existence, as Goethe observes, who daily conquer them anew.[39] If we are to develop our individuality we

[34]Frankl, *Man's Search for Meaning*, pp. 136-37.

[35]Arnold and Gasson, *The Human Person*, p. 469.

[36]Rollo May, ed., *Existential Psychology* (New York: Random House, 1961), pp. 41, 44.

[37]Rollo May, Ernest Angel, and Henri F. Ellenberger, eds., *Existence: A New Dimension in Psychiatry and Psychology*, A Clarion Book. (New York: Simon and Schuster, 1958), p. 71.

[38]Rollo May, *The Art of Counseling*, Apex Books. (New York: Abingdon Press, 1939), pp. 45, 51.

[39]Rollo May, *Psychology and the Human Dilemma* (Princeton, New Jersey: D. VanNostrand Company, 1967), pp. 140, 168, 176-78.

must drop all pretenses, quit our role playing, and develop ourselves into that which we are. When "we find our real selves," we "find our society" by relating properly to others, and in a sense, we also find God.[40]

The more socially integrated we become, the more we are able, on the whole, to realize our unique personalities. We are able as healthy persons increasingly to realize and accept our social responsibility. Our striving to overcome feelings of inferiority is now directed toward socially constructive ends.[41]

Dealing with our religious tensions is of central importance. We all have conflict, feelings of oughtness, a sense of discrepancy between what we are or do and what we ought to be or do, or between an ideal perfection and our own imperfection. We must learn to live with the tension of inevitable guilt feelings arising because of this gap. On the other hand, we must be freed from morbid guilt feelings and guilt because of sin. We implore God for freedom from the unbearable bondage of egocentricity and sin; without His grace we remain in our sinful predicament.[42]

Our essential condition is that of emptiness, loneliness and anxiety. We are the "hollow people" about whom T. S. Eliot wrote a third of a century ago. Lacking an autonomy and power amid life's circumstances, we are a far cry from Riesman's *inner*-directed persons, with strong motives, morals and ambitions, stabilized by an inner gyroscope. Instead, we are *outer*-directed persons, adjusting to life by having radar sets fastened to our heads to tell us what others expect of us.[43] We are able to respond, but not to choose. Having no effective center of motivation of our own, we are characterized by apathy, loneliness, alienation and anxiety. Desperately afraid in our moments of solitude, we are anxious because we

---

[40]May, *The Art of Counseling*, p. 61.

[41]*Ibid.*, pp. 64, 67.

[42]*Ibid.*, pp. 70-74; 219-23.

[43]David Riesman, Nathan Glazer and Reuel Denney, *The Lonely Crowd: A Study of the Changing American Character* (New York: Doubleday and Company, 1953), pp. 32, 48.

do not know what principles for action to believe in nor what rules to pursue. We resemble Willie Loman in Arthur Miller's *Death of a Salesman*, who "never knew who he was."[44]

There are tragic developments which have led us to our existential situation, May contends.[45] We have lost, for one thing, the central values of our society; the old values and goals are in a state of transition. Also, we have lost a sense of self. While having gained confidence in gadgets and technology, we have lost faith in ourselves as persons. Finally, we have lost our language for personal communication; we can no longer communicate that which has deep personal meaning to us. We must regain that ability to affirm ourselves as persons, despite the changing technology and the impersonality of others and of nature.

MAN IN CHRISTIAN PERSPECTIVE

Having completed an overview of several major approaches to the problem of the nature of man, we are now ready to set forth a Christian perspective. While it appears that frequently, as "natural" or unredeemed persons, we are unable or refuse to recognize evil propensities within ourselves, it is obvious that many of us as Christians fail to see enough good in our unregenerate fellowman. What we need, then, in a Christian perspective, is a synthesis of these two positions. Theologians, it would seem, have told us the truth, but unfortunately, they have not told us the *whole* truth.

As children, we have outbursts of temper; almost universally we lie and, more frequently than we want to admit, cheat, steal and destroy. But as children we are *good*, also. We show great faith and trust in those we love, we are accepting and loving toward people generally, we delight in our surroundings, are utterly sincere and quick to forgive those who wrong us. Both good and evil abound in our childish

---

[44]Rollo May, *Man's Search for Himself*, A Signet Book. (New York: The New American Library, 1953), pp. 15-19, 23-24, 30-33, 44.
[45]*Ibid.*, pp. 41-64.

natures; we are ambivalent; contradiction is more evident than any form of consistency.

We carry, figuratively, the seeds of both good and evil within. Training and example, therefore, assume momentous significance. Love and affection as well as firmness and consistency in discipline are necessary to provide the proper growing ground so that we will smoothly internalize this good training. Surrounded by what is good and right, our decision to accept the way of Christ can become almost a "natural" one. By "natural" we do not mean that the child grows into the Christian life, of course. But, just as childbirth is preceded by prenatal growth and development, we may be trained and nurtured so that our spiritual birth is greatly facilitated.

Our approach to the nature of man, then, is not one of "either-or" but of "both-and." Man is good and bad; depraved yet made in the image of God. That we have an evil side to our nature would seem to be an incontrovertible fact of existence, thoroughly verifiable by Scripture. "I don't accomplish the good I set out to do," St. Paul admits, "and the evil I don't really want to do I find I am always doing. . . . Who on earth can set me free from the clutches of *my own sinful nature?*" (Romans 7:19, 24, Phillips). Again, he declares, "Everyone has sinned; everyone falls short of the beauty of God's plan" (Romans 3:23, Phillips).

Christ knows what is inside us in our unconverted state. On the one hand, He recognizes that in such a state we can travel a great distance on our own. We are able to cultivate ourselves so as to be completely exemplary even from a moral and religious standpoint. Saul of Tarsus and Nicodemus are two cases in point. Yet when Paul sees himself as Christ sees him, he calls himself the chief of sinners. Nicodemus, likewise an outstanding scholar and teacher in the most conservative religious tradition of his day, hears Christ say to him, "A man cannot even see the kingdom of God without being born again. . . . You must be born again" (John 3:3, 7, Phillips). Something is fundamentally wrong at the core of our nature, and Christ's all-seeing look focuses upon

tion upon the concepts of conscience and guilt. Rushdoony, while generally critical of Freudian thought, acknowledges that no man outside the realm of Christian scholarship has faced the guilt question any more openly and plainly than Freud.

Freud declares the sense of guilt to be the most important problem in the evolution of our culture. No matter what marvels scientific technology may bring forth, if we are over-powered by guilt we are miserable amid riches. Before anything else can be done for us, therefore, we must reckon with the fact of guilt. Freud faces this issue as a scientist, so that instead of confronting such theological aspects as God, creation and the "Fall of Man," he approaches the subject of guilt anthropologically.[2] It is unfortunate that in most conservative Christian circles Freud and psychoanalysis have been generally "rejected without a hearing." Many of us have been content to read secondary sources highly critical of him, and to be closed-minded relative to any beneficial effects that psychoanalytic thinking might have upon us or our Christian philosophy.

Freud's anthropological explanation of guilt has done little to establish him in the good graces of orthodox Christians, even though his study leads him to conclude that "we are all miserable sinners." He quotes with favor Atkinson's theory of the beginning of life:[3]

> There is a violent and jealous father who keeps all the females for himself and drives away his sons as they grow up. . . . One day the brothers who had been driven out came together, killed and devoured their father and so made an end of the patriarchal horde. . . .
>
> The tumultuous mob of brothers were filled with . . . contradictory feelings. . . . They hated their father, who presented such a formidable obstacle to their craving for

[2]Rousas J. Rushdoony, *Freud*, Modern Thinkers Series. (Philadelphia: Presbyterian and Reformed Publishing Company, 1965), p. 20.
[3]Freud, Sigmund, *Totem and Taboo*, trans. by James Strachey. (New York: W. W. Norton and Company, 1950), pp. 72, 141-43.

power and their sexual desires; but they loved and admired him too. After they had got rid of him . . . the affection which had all this time been pushed under was bound to make itself felt. It did so in the form of remorse. A sense of guilt made its appearance, which in this instance coincided with the remorse felt by the whole group. The dead father became stronger than the living one had been. . . . What had up to then been prevented by his actual existence was thenceforward prohibited by the sons themselves. . . . They revoked their deed by forbidding the killing of the totem, the substitute for their father; and they renounced its fruits by resigning their claim to the women who had now been set free. They thus created out of their filial sense of guilt the two fundamental taboos of totemism. . . . Whoever contravened those taboos became guilty of the only two crimes with which primitive society concerned itself.

Freud recognizes three varieties of anxiety: reality, neurotic and moral. Reality anxiety is the fear of real dangers present in the external world, neurotic anxiety is the fear that we cannot control our instincts and will do something worthy of punishment, while moral anxiety is the fear of the conscience. We tend to feel "conscience stricken" whenever we do something or even think of doing something contrary to the moral code by which we have been raised. Moral anxiety also has a realistic basis: we have been punished in the past for violating the moral code and may be punished again.[4] Our moral sense of guilt is the expression of the tension between the attainments of the ego and the demands of the superego.[5]

Freud elaborates further upon the roles of the ego and superego (roughly equivalent to the self and the conscience, respectively).[6] Our ego is formed to a large extent out of

[4]Hall and Lindzey, *Theories of Personality*, p. 45.
[5]Sigmund Freud, *New Introductory Lectures on Psycho-Analysis*, trans. by W. J. H. Sprott. (New York: W. W. Norton and Company, 1933), p. 88.
[6]Sigmund Freud, "The Ego and the Id," in *A General Selection from the Works of Sigmund Freud*, ed. by John Rickman. (New York: Liveright Publishing Corporation, 1957), pp. 227-28.

identifications, the earliest of which stand apart from the remainder of the ego in the form of the superego. Later, as it grows stronger, the ego becomes more able to withstand the effects of such identifications. Although our superego is amenable to all later influences, it preserves throughout life the capacity to stand apart from the ego and rule over it. Even the mature ego remains subject to its domination.

Because Freud reasons from naturalistic presuppositions, he does not accept the roles of freedom, autonomy and responsibility in personality. Nor does he postulate a sense of sin that can be remedied by repentance. It is not misdeeds but *impulses* that cause guilt feelings, which in turn may lead to neurosis. If we inquire among neurotics to discover what deeds provoke guilt we shall be disappointed; we find no deeds, only impulses and emotions, set upon evil ends, but never achieved. What lie behind the sense of guilt of neurotics are invariably *psychic* realities, never *actual* ones. He does point out, however, that such a sense of guilt has some justification, for it is founded on the intense and frequent, yet unconscious, wishes for the death of certain of our fellow-men.[7]

It is a short step from the discovery that unfulfilled impulses can cause severe neuroticism to the viewpoint that the superego is unduly demanding. We are faced with a picture, clinically speaking, of a superego that is severe, even cruel. Experience shows that this superego may demonstrate a relentless harshness even when our upbringing has been gentle and kind, and threats and punishments have been carefully avoided.[8] For Freud, guilt is viewed as highly abnormal, and the cause of serious emotional problems. It is logical that he, studying extensively his patients' sexual behavior, should look upon guilt in this manner, for nineteenth century society is renowned for its having attached a great amount of guilt to nearly all sexual phenomena.[9]

Freud hypothesizes that the greater part of guilt is uncon-

---

[7]Freud, *Totem and Taboo*, pp. 86-87.
[8]Freud, *New Introductory Lectures*, pp. 87, 90.
[9]May, *The Art of Counseling*, p. 70.

scious and therefore causes serious behavior problems, even criminal and masochistic (self-punishing) acts.[10] Aggravation of unconscious guilt turns many people into criminals. In youthful offenders, especially, a powerful sense of guilt is found to exist before their crimes and to serve as their motive. It is as if they have to fasten their unconscious sense of guilt upon something real and immediate. Guilt feeling may also lead to a masochistic tendency. If a psychoanalytic solution of a symptom is accomplished, that symptom should disappear. But in masochistic persons, there is a momentary intensification of the symptom. Lacking the will to recover, they favor illness with its attendant suffering and handicaps. Because the sense of guilt finds relief and atonement in the illness, masochists refuse to give up their suffering. The sense of guilt expresses itself, then, as a resistance to recovery. This unconscious need for punishment is seen by Freud as an aggressiveness set up against the parents for which it can find no outward discharge.

The two basic objectives in psychoanalytic therapy are to reduce the power of the superego and to increase ego strength. To reduce the force of the superego is to reduce internal controls and free the personality of inhibitions. The rapist, e.g., encouraged to feel "good" about his crime, is in effect told: "go and sin some more." The goal of increasing ego strength is complementary to superego reduction, for the ego can hardly gain strength at the expense of the id, since instincts cannot be modified. It grows, therefore, at the expense of the superego and further reduces the power of conscience to punish and control unlawful behavior. Both objectives, then, if achieved, reduce controls on behavior.[11]

Carl Jung

The concept of guilt does not receive the centrality of emphasis in Jung that it enjoys in Freud. His cure for neuro-

---

[10]Freud, "The Ego and the Id," pp. 228, 230-31.
[11]James W. Wiggins, "Criminology and the Sick Society," in *Morality and Mental Health*, ed. by O. Hobart Mowrer. (Chicago: Rand McNally and Company, 1967), p. 551.

sis and meaninglessness is not tied to a concept of guilt.
We have heard altogether too much about guilt and sin, Jung
contends. We are sorely enough beset by our own bad
conscience, and want to learn rather how we may be reconciled with our own nature. Therapists are to help us accept
the evil side of our nature as a true ally, for only in so doing
can we truly understand ourselves. To accomplish this feat
is to reunite the contradictory elements of the personality
and bring to an end the inner "civil war." We should avoid
the extremes of identifying ourselves completely with the
new, or running away altogether from the past. To do either
is to salvage only a narrow state of consciousness. Instead,
we must be willing to live in the tension inherent in the play
of opposites within, and thus build up a state of wider and
higher consciousness. Becoming aware, then, of our divided
state is an essential step in our well-being.[12]

Despite these contentions, Jung insists[13] that we are products of original sin, a condition grossly underestimated even
by theologians. Simply because we have busily denied our
evil nature, adding stupidity to iniquity, none of our evil
deeds has disappeared. We are guilty of sins and bear indeli-
bly within us the capacity and inclination to do them again
at any time. Evil "bestrides the psychological stage" as an
equal or opposite partner of good, in a psychological dual-
ism.

Our unconscious, while a dangerous opponent, is also the
source of highest spiritual good. Guidance comes from God,
who is an archetype lodged in the deepest levels of our collective unconscious.[14] The experience of the God-image
or archetype is the most vital and overwhelming available to
human beings.[15] We become neurotic because we have not

---

[12]Carl G. Jung, *Modern Man in Search of a Soul*, trans. by W. S.
Dell and Cary F. Baynes. (New York: Harcourt, Brace and Company, 1933), pp. 114-17, 274-75.
[13]Carl G. Jung, *The Undiscovered Self*, trans. by R. F. C. Hull.
(Boston: Little Brown and Company, 1957), pp. 95-98.
[14]Jung, *Modern Man in Search of a Soul*, pp. 279-80.
[15]Freida Fordham, *An Introduction to Jung's Psychology*, A Pelican Original. (Baltimore: Penguin Books, 1953), p. 73.

found true meaning in life. We are ill because we have no love, only sexuality; no faith, because we are afraid to grope in the dark; no hope, because we are disillusioned by the world and by life; and no understanding, because we have failed to read the meaning of our own existence.[16] We can be cured by finding our way back to the church or by experiencing a conversion; but such solutions cannot be imposed from without; they must come from a sense of inner need. The need for analytic treatment is dictated because of our use of that old psychological mechanism, repression. Once our human mind has succeeded in inventing the idea of sin, repression arises. And because we conceal acts, we alienate ourselves from the community. What is concealed tends to be the dark, imperfect and stupid in ourselves, so our secrets are laden with guilt, whether or not they are really wrong from the standpoint of conventional morality. Full confession, releasing these suppressed emotions, may be expected to bring about an appreciable healing effect.[17]

Jung's other unique contributions come, first, in his insistence that neurosis is not something entirely negative, but, if properly viewed, may lead to new possibilities of development; and second, in his view that there are other important drives in human nature besides sexuality and self-assertion, and that the cultural or spiritual drive, dominant in the second half of life, is of greater importance than either of the other two.[18]

Otto Rank

Of all of the psychoanalysts, Rank has most clearly grasped the relationship between religion and psychology. His writings are not readily understood, however — in part due to his somewhat incomprehensible writing style, but also because his thinking undergoes such a dramatic change over a lifetime that he appears to contradict himself on occasion.

---

[16]Jung, *Modern Man in Search of a Soul*, p. 260.
[17]Fordham, *An Introduction to Jung's Psychology*, pp. 76, 89-90.
[18]*Ibid.*, p. 88.

Much of his earlier thinking is reactionary to Freud's, but
later emerges as a penetrating and comprehensive viewpoint
of psychology. His style, while, on the one hand, frequently
critical and negative, is, on the other, that of a sensitive
artist attempting to convey at least something of the framework of his own religious experience.[19]

His later thought draws upon the implications of Adler
and Jung as well as his own wide background of study regarding the historical and anthropological perspectives of
psychology and psychoanalysis. He concludes that psychoanalysis has assumed a supplanting function, substituting psy-
choanalytical interpretations for traditional religious teachings. Rationalistic explanations of human existence cannot
possibly solve our problems since our lives inconveniently refuse to follow rational patterns. Our basic need is to re-establish a relationship with the creative forces of life. Psychoanalysis cannot produce the spontaneity of creative acts so
essential in works of art and in religious faith as well as in the
meaningful experiencing of everyday life. It is this insight of
Rank's that may be credited with propelling psychology in a
new direction, namely, toward the search for *meaning*. Only
the experiencing of meaningfulness in life can make us whole
persons.[20]

Rank makes explicit this meaningfulness through his
"will to immortality," a concept evolving out of his analysis of
four historical stages of belief in immortality.[21] The stages
are the "animistic" (or primitive), the "spiritual," the "sexual"
and the "psychological." He ties these stages with his understanding of the human will. Interpreting the expression of the
will in the perspective of history, he attempts to demonstrate, first, that the fundamental conceptions that underlie our
beliefs about life have their sources beyond consciousness
and rationality, and, second, that these deepest, unconscious,
most intimately assumed beliefs about life have varied with

---

[19]Ira Progoff, *The Death and Rebirth of Psychology* (New York:
The Julian Press, 1956), pp. 189-90.
[20]*Ibid.*, pp. 11-12, 15.
[21]*Ibid.*, pp. 209, 215.

the development of history. The modern personality, then, can be understood best in an expansive, historical perspective of our psychological development as a race.

Rank traces the concept of "will as evil" back to early Christianity, where the reward for being good or evil eventuates in either immortality or death for the soul. In the pre-Christian era, bad will and positive, active will are synonymous. Will is a subjective power within us, "evil, guilty, and morally damned." Since will power corresponds to life power (mana), the result of condemning willing as a bad power leads to a negation of life itself. Because some have projected their bad will power onto others, or the dead, or even God — the will has become labeled as bad in itself.[22]

Freud's stance on sexuality is that it is an instinctual and therefore universal part of human nature. Rank, on the other hand, insists[23] that for primitive men sexual contact had not become important enough to be an object of guilt feelings and taboos. Looking upon sex at that time as merely play, it was only in a later stage of evolution that men "discovered sexuality." Sexual intercourse, in that stage of history, was not understood as resulting in reproduction, but was looked upon only as an act of pleasure to which they gave themselves under appropriate circumstances and at certain times.

Only in the "sexual" era does sex become important enough to be associated with guilt. The "naive, playful" activity of the "pre-sexual" era becomes, in the "sexual" era, taboo, and is hemmed about by restrictions and ritualism that control it while exalting it as the center of society's way of life. Sexuality becomes restricted to "impregnation for the sake of begetting children and achieving reproductive immortality." Indulgence in sexual activity for any other purpose is looked upon as sin.[24] Thus we see that the great affirmative force of sexual energies has become negative and burdened

---

[22]Otto Rank, *Psychology and the Soul*, trans. by William D. Turner. (Philadelphia: University of Pennsylvania Press, 1950), pp. 162, 164.

[23]Progoff, *Death and Rebirth*, pp. 216-17.

[24]Rank, *Psychology and the Soul*, p. 39.

down with guilt feelings. The road to immortality has become highly uncertain, for we are caught in the confusion between sexuality and our belief in the soul.[25]

As an expression of will, sexuality has become evil, guilty and a cause of death, characteristics formerly ascribed to the *will*. Since will can actually bring about death[26] it has become bad in itself. But to label it such does not cause it to disappear. Instead, it becomes transformed into a negative power interpreted as guilt feeling, and, as such, linked with sin. So the "age of psychology" inherits a broken, denied will and the moral phenomenon of guilt which now lacks its former connotations of power. Also, the belief in immortality has been replaced by an anxiety over death. Thus the "psychological" era is born of weakness and in a sense, death — the death of the old beliefs formerly so meaningful.[27]

The negative quality of psychology is clearly shown in the fact that it is capable of explaining but never of believing. Psychological truth remains basically and paradoxically an absence of belief, and its negativistic nature extends as far as to our fundamental ideology — the belief in the immortality of the soul. Only in the psychological era has our belief in immortality lost, to a significant degree, its inspirational force. Psychology is a destroyer of illusions and ideologies which cannot withstand progressive self-consciousness. Increasingly unable to maintain even itself, however, it finally destroys itself.[28]

Rank's total frame of reference contrasts with Freud's "world as a machine" concept. Rank tends to be integrative, constructive, and appreciative in his approach to cultural phenomena, in contrast to Freud's analytical, reductive and deprecative approach.[29] Freud emphasizes external restric-

---

[25]Progoff, *Death and Rebirth*, pp. 220-21.
[26]In the primitive era men could cause the death of others by projecting their 'bad will' upon them. See Rank's *Psychology and the Soul*, pp. 160-61.
[27]Rank, *Psychology and the Soul*, pp. 164-65.
[28]*Ibid.*, pp. 192-93.
[29]Fay B. Karpf, *The Psychology and Psychotherapy of Otto Rank* (New York: Philosophical Library, 1953), pp. 107, 109.

tions and deprivations (punishment and reward), while Rank considers the inner voice of our conscience much more reliable.[30] Rank displays little patience with Freud's idea that guilt can be diagnosed or rationalized out of existence. He scoffs at Freud's naiveté and presumptuousness in thinking that we can remove guilt by explaining it casually as neurotic, and his attempt to explain old spiritual beliefs in terms of their sexual origins as if to neutralize them and thus reduce conflict between sexual and spiritual ideologies.[31]

Rank uniquely utilizes two great therapeutic principles, love and force. A constructive therapy will not attempt to alter us but bring us to the place where we can accept ourselves as we are. As patients we implement the love principle by agreeing with and subjecting ourselves to the therapist's will. The force principle conversely becomes the means of asserting our will against the therapist's. Both lead to a rise of guilt feelings. The first is the guilt over a lack of creativity, which is a basic need not being met because of our acquiescence to the therapist. The second is the consciousness of guilt that follows the realization that we should not have this "wicked counter will." While guilt consciousness works repressively and destructively within, and therefore needs to be acknowledged and dealt with in therapy, the guilt following creativeness operates progressively and constructively, spurring us on to newer and higher achievements of will. The only escape, then, from the guilt conflict is to let us create for ourselves our own development and our own freeing.[32]

The creative will automatically brings guilt with it. Will and guilt are two sides of the same coin. Free will belongs to the idea of guilt and sin as inevitably as day belongs to night. We are guilty psychologically and feel ourselves responsible, and no psychoanalysis can relieve us of this guilt feeling.

---

[30]Otto Rank, *Beyond Psychology* (New York: Dover Publications, 1958), p. 274.

[31]Progoff, *Death and Rebirth*, pp. 222-23.

[32]Otto Rank, *Will Therapy and Truth and Reality*, trans. by Jessie Taft. (New York: Alfred A. Knopf, 1964), pp. 65-67.

We should be guided, then, so that we may constructively face the results of our willing — inevitable guilt feeling.[33]

In his mature thinking, Rank attempts to overcome the weaknesses of his own psychology of consciousness and Freud's instinctual drives by proposing a "third principle."[34] As moderns, we do not act exclusively upon the rational guidance of our intellectual ego, nor are we driven blindly by the elemental forces of our instinctual self. There is a synthesizing principle, a "will to immortality," which, despite the deprecations of anthropologists and psychologists, stands as the chief link between ourselves and our remote ancestors.

The road *beyond psychology* leads to a point where art and religion meet, join and transform each other. If as creative persons we are to fulfill the meaning of our lives and play a heroic role in the modern world, we must take the lead in going beyond the present "transitional psycho-therapeutic stage." By experiencing the reality of immortality moment by moment we shall create a new life for ourselves, even as St. Paul did on the Damascus Road.[35] It is a life of which all may partake. Being "twice-born" himself, Paul becomes the prototype for *all* mankind. And each of us, by participating in Christ's resurrection, may be "twice-born" in this present life.[36]

A LOOK AT NEO-ANALYTIC THEORISTS

Karen Horney

The results of her work in the field of neurosis lead Horney to frequent disagreements with Freud. Difficulties of human personality arise, she maintains, not from conflicts between ego, id and superego, i.e., determined by heredity, as Freud contends, but from conflicts between us and our environment.[37] Conflicts are avoidable or resolvable if we have been

---

[33]*Ibid.*, pp. 239-40.
[34]Rank, *Beyond Psychology*, pp. 62-63.
[35]Progoff, *Death and Rebirth*, pp. 251-52.
[36]Rank, *Beyond Psychology*, pp. 159-61.
[37]Floyd L. Ruch, *Psychology and Life* (7th ed.; Chicago: Scott, Foresman and Company, 1963), p. 121.

raised with warmth and love, but where these have been lacking, neurotic trends will begin. While as children we may experience hostility toward one or both parents, we repress it because of helplessness, fear, love or feelings of guilt. Because neurotic tendencies are not instinctual, but spring from disturbed human relationships, they can be corrected when such relationships are improved.[38]

Horney discusses at length the reasons neurotics are so frequently afflicted with debilitating guilt feelings. She rejects Freud's contentions that unconscious guilt *feelings* are the cause of neurosis as well as his observation that neurotics are no more immoral than others, but simply *feel more guilty*. She avows that as neurotics our need is to appear "perfect" and "right" before the therapist (indeed, before everyone). Even while we are seeking help, we are convinced that we are right — and this is our rudimentary problem. In therapy we must see that our basic problem is the outlandishness of our perfectionism; we are simply demanding the impossible of ourselves.[39]

Horney, in dealing with the manifestations of guilt feelings, presents us with a frightening array of symptoms that are induced by guilt.[40] Her conviction that guilt feelings play a central role in neurosis comes about not so much through the observation of comparatively infrequent *direct* expressions (such as feelings of unworthiness, or fantasies concerning incest with and death wishes of "loved ones"), but the more frequently encountered *indirect* expressions — self-recriminations which concern everything and everyone, hypersensitivity over disapproval by others, a fear of being "found out," and a tendency to invite adverse happenings.

Repression is cited by Horney as one of two major evils precipitating our neurosis.[41] Our need to appear perfect

---

[38]Karen Horney, *Our Inner Conflicts* (New York: W. W. Norton and Company, 1945), p. 187.

[39]Karen Horney, *New Ways in Psychoanalysis* (New York: W. W. Norton and Company, 1939), pp. 235, 238, 244-45.

[40]*Ibid.*, pp. 232-35.

[41]*Ibid.*, pp. 229, 237-40.

leads to the repressing of, first, everything that does not fit
into our particular façade and, second, everything that would
render it impossible for us to maintain that stance. As per-
fectionistic persons, we are deeply afraid of anyone recognizing our façade for what it is, "phoniness." Our standards
are simply a "front" designed to serve the particular purpose
of appearing perfect.

The other trouble-maker, along with repression, is the phenomenon of unattached guilt feelings. We feel haunted by
such feelings without being able to attach them to anything
tangible. Sometimes a more concrete ·self-accusation will
emerge and we feel that now we have found the reason that
we hate ourselves. Tragically, while we are aware of the results of self-hate (feeling guilty, inferior, cramped, torment-
ed) we have no realization that we have brought these painful feelings upon ourselves. And even the bit of awareness
we may have frequently is blurred by neurotic pride. Instead
of suffering from this condition, we are proud of being unselfish or ascetic or self-sacrificing or a slave to duty.[42]

Erich Fromm

Fromm's penetrating analysis of our human condition is
strongly humanistic. He observes that our freedom, while
appearing to be desirable, has become our downfall. We
feel lonely and isolated because we have become separated
from nature and others. As we mature, we gain freedom
from our primary ties (parents), with the result that we feel
isolated and helpless. Although gaining more freedom through
the centuries, we have felt increasingly alone. Freedom thus
becomes a negative state from which we try to escape.
Fromm's positive solution to this dilemma is that we unite
ourselves with others spontaneously in a spirit of love or sharing of work, and thus preserve our hard-won freedom. The
alternative so frequently taken is to submit to authority and
conform to the expectations of society, which results in se-

[42]Karen Horney, *Neurosis and Human Growth* (New York: W.
W. Norton and Company, 1950), pp. 116, 128-29.

curity, but brings with it new bondage. Our adjustment to society usually represents a compromise between inner needs and outer demands. We develop a social character in keeping with the requirements of society. Fromm contends that both capitalism and communism, by making demands upon us that are contrary to our nature, warp and frustrate us.[43]

One of the major effects of capitalism upon personality is alienation. Alienated persons cannot possibly be healthy. Experiencing ourselves as things to be manipulated we lack a sense of self, and develop deep anxiety. We feel inferior whenever we suspect that we are not "lining up." But because we are humans we cannot help deviating, so we live in the constant fear of disapproval. The other result of alienation is the feeling of guilt. We find that, beneath the surface, we feel guilty about hundreds of things: for not having worked diligently enough, for having been overprotective — or underprotective — toward our children; for having done good things, or bad; for being ourselves and not being ourselves; it is almost as if we have to find something about which to feel guilty.

There are two main explanations for all this guilt feeling. First, it is traceable to the same source as inferiority feeling. Not to be exactly like the rest, or "totally" adjusted, makes us feel guilty. The second source is our conscience: we sense our talents, our ability to love, think, cry, laugh, wonder and create, and that our life is the one chance we are given, and to lose this chance is to lose everything.[44]

Fromm is highly critical of parents for fostering guilt feelings within us as children when our actions do not please them.[45] We feel guilty for not loving our parents sufficiently, especially when they expect to be the focus of our feelings. At other times we feel guilty over having disappointed them in their expectations for us. Many parents feel that children

---

[43]Hall and Lindzey, *Theories of Personality*, pp. 127-29.

[44]Erich Fromm, *The Sane Society* (New York: Rinehart and Company, 1955), pp. 124, 205.

[45]Fromm, *Man for Himself*, pp. 153-56.

are brought into the world to satisfy them and to compensate them for whatever disappointments enter their lives.

Frequently parents want us to be "serviceable." Unsuccessful themselves, they expect us to attain success so they may feel a vicarious satisfaction. If they do not feel loved we are to compensate for it. Dominating parents demand that we be like them in temperament and character. Failure to do so brings a guilty conscience. Attempts to free ourselves from such notions of obligation and become "ourselves" may exact a heavy toll of guilt.

Not only do guilt feelings result from our dependence upon irrational authority and the feeling that it is our duty to please that authority, but the guilt feeling in turn reinforces our dependence. Guilt feelings have been proven to be the most effective means of forming and increasing dependency. The authority (parent or otherwise) makes us feel guilty for our many transgressions. The guilt over these and the need for their forgiveness creates an endless chain of offense, guilt feeling, and the need for absolution, which keeps us in bondage as well as grateful for forgiveness, rather than critical of the authority's demands.

The most effective method for weakening our will is to arouse our sense of guilt, which is done by making us feel that our early sexual explorations are "naughty." Since we cannot help having these strivings, this method of arousing guilt can hardly fail. By age five or six we have thus acquired an all-pervasive sense of guilt.

Inasmuch as this "irrational" social and parental authority tends to break our will, spontaneity and independence, we fight against it — and fight for ourselves as full-fledged human beings. Few of us succeed entirely. The scars left from our defeats are to be found at the root of every neurosis. They comprise a syndrome: the weakening or paralysis of our originality and spontaneity; the weakening of the true self and its replacement by a pseudo-self in which the feeling of "I am" is dulled and substituted by the experience of the "self as the sum total of others' expectations"; the substitution of autonomy by heteronomy; and the fogginess of our interpersonal experiences. The most pronounced symptom of the defeat in the fight for self is the guilty conscience.[46]

Fromm observes two consciences among us; the authoritarian and the humanistic. In authoritarian religion, sin is essentially disobedience to authority, and, only secondarily, violation of ethical norms.[47] Our authoritarian conscience is derived from the commandments and taboos of the authority; its strength is expressed in the emotions of fear and/or admiration toward the authority. A good conscience comes from pleasing the authority; a guilty conscience from displeasing it. Inner security comes by becoming identified with that which is more powerful than ourselves.[48]

Will is a form of rebellion against the authority's prerogatives. It produces guilt, which, in turn, reduces our power, increases our submission, and keeps us from becoming our own "creator and builder." To have sinned means to have disobeyed powerful authorities who will punish us. Acts of rebellion can be atoned for only by submission. To feel guilty is to feel depraved and powerless, and thus throw ourselves completely on the mercy of the authority for forgiveness.[49] The result is that we are morally weakened, filled with self-hate and disgust, and thus prone to sin again when we are over our "orgy of self-flagellation."[50]

In humanistic religion we find an entirely different reaction to sin. Lacking the spirit of hate and intolerance, our tendency to violate living norms is looked upon with understanding and love, not scorn and contempt. To be aware of our sins means to experience the totality of our own powers, not a sense of powerlessness. Conscience is not the internalized voice of authority, but our own voice, the guardian of our integrity which brings us back to ourselves when we are in

---

[46]*Ibid.*, pp. 157-58.

[47]Erich Fromm, *Psychoanalysis and Religion* (New Haven: Yale University Press, 1950), p. 88.

[48]Fromm, *Man for Himself*, p. 146.

[49]*Ibid.*, p. 150.

[50]Fromm, *Psychoanalysis and Religion*, pp. 88-89.

great danger of losing ourselves. Present in all of us, it is independent of external sanctions or rewards.[51]

The "good" conscience operates when actions, thoughts and feelings, conducive to the proper functioning and unfolding of our total personality, produce a feeling of inner approval, of "rightness." Conversely, acts, thoughts and feelings injurious to our total personality produce feelings of uneasiness, discomfort and a "guilty" conscience. Conscience is thus the reaction of ourselves to ourselves. It is the voice which summons us back to ourselves, to live productively, to develop fully and harmoniously; i.e., to become what we potentially are.[52]

A Look at Existentialists

Viktor Frankl

Frankl's "will-to-meaning" stands in contrast to Freud's pleasure principle and Adler's power principle, but somewhat resembles Rank's "will to immortality." Maintaining that every generation has its own collective neurosis, Frankl declares that the existential vacuum is the mass neurosis of our age. The attempt to find meaning in society as well as in our individual lives is the great thrust of Frankl's logotherapy. The concept of existential neurosis involves the recognition of a truly spiritual dimension of personality. Illnesses arise not so much from repressed traumatic experiences or stress-producing situations, but from our inability to see meaning in life, so that we are living inauthentically, or as he phrases it, "an inauthentic existential modality." Our problem is to find meaning in living and thus to assume an "authentic modality of existence."[53]

While Frankl insists that there is a widespread noögenic neurosis that takes root in lives lived meaninglessly, he underscores the clinical fact that it is not tension, stress and conflict per se that cause mental illness.[54] In innumerable in-

---

[51]Ibid.
[52]Fromm, Man for Himself, p. 159.
[53]May, Angel, and Ellenberger, eds., Existence, p. 119.
[54]Tweedie, The Christian and the Couch, pp. 94-95.

stances, concentration camp inmates endure all of the pressures and stresses of imprisonment only to break down after liberation. We become ill because a sense of meaninglessness becomes overpowering in our lives, and we lack the inner resources to combat it.

To achieve mental health, Frankl stresses the importance of dealing effectively with life's inherent tensions, a point also made by Rollo May and Otto Rank. We should not be hesitant about challenging man with a potential meaning for him to fulfill. What we need as human beings — and especially as neurotics — is not homeostasis, but noödynamics, i.e., the spiritual dynamic in a polar field of tension where one pole is represented by meanings to be fulfilled and the other by persons who must fulfill them.[55]

While it might seem futile, from a utilitarian point of view, to repent of past wrong-doing, repentance has meaning. It has the power to wipe out a wrong; for though that wrong cannot be undone, the penitent undergoes a moral rebirth. Guilt presupposes responsibility. We are responsible in the sense that we cannot retrace a single step; every decision, small or large, remains a final one. None of our acts of commission or omission may be wiped off the slate as if they had never happened. But in repenting we may inwardly break with an act, and in living out our repentance (an inner event) we can "undo the outer event on a spiritual, moral plane."[56]

We look in vain for a biblical presentation of the place of guilt in Frankl's writings. He is not unaware of the significance of guilt in therapy, but simply presents it as a basic human problem without considering it as the judgment of God. Its alleviation is not considered, therefore, to be particularly different from the alleviation of any psychodynamic problem.[57]

Frankl frequently takes note, however, of the role of guilt in the various neuroses. He maintains, e.g., that in hypochondriachal anxiety, we have a derivative of existential anxi-

[55]Frankl, *Man's Search for Meaning*, pp. 106-07.
[56]Frankl, *The Doctor and the Soul*, pp. 108-09.
[57]Tweedie, *Logotherapy and the Christian Faith*, p. 167.

ety applied to a single organ in the body. The fear of death, experienced because we have a guilty conscience toward life, is pushed out of consciousness only to become localized in a particular organ.[58] Similarly, he makes other references to guilt as it pertains to those suffering from endogenous depression, obsessive-compulsive neuroses, and melancholic symptoms.

We do not find in Frankl's writings a strong case for guilt developing in relationship to God in the moral sense. The exception: one reference is made to the fact that the conscientious anxiety of the overscrupulous person is experienced in the melancholic as a sense of inadequacy centering around the question of *moral righteousness*.[59]

Rollo May

Psychotherapy has failed to take the matter of guilt seriously enough, says Rollo May, who takes an existential approach to the problem of guilt which cuts through what he calls the dense fog obscuring much of the discussion on this subject. Such discussion typically has proceeded on the assumption that we can only deal with some vague "guilt feelings," as if whether guilt is real or not is of little significance.[60]

May sees anxiety and guilt as inextricably intertwined; to experience anxiety is to experience the threat of imminent non-being. It is becoming aware that our existence can be destroyed, that we can lose ourselves and our world and become nothing. Anxiety always involves inner conflict. If there were not some new possibility before us we would not experience anxiety. Anxiety, then, is connected with the problem of freedom. Once we become aware of opportunities and then fail to avail ourselves of them, guilt is inevitable.[61]

Rollo May delineates three forms of ontological guilt.[62] The first, *Eigenwelt* ("own world") is that which arises from

[58]Frankl, *The Doctor and the Soul*, pp. 179-80.
[59]*Ibid.*, p. 203.
[60]May, Angel and Ellenberger, eds., *Existence*, p. 54.
[61]*Ibid.*, pp. 50, 52.
[62]*Ibid.*, pp. 54-55.

forfeiting our possibilities, locking them up within ourselves. A second form of guilt arises from the fact that because we are human we necessarily perceive our fellow man through limited and biased eyes. We always do at least some violence to the true picture of our fellows and fail to some extent to understand and meet their needs. This is not a problem of moral failure or slackness, although a keen sensitivity in the moral realm helps. It is an inescapable result of the fact that we look at the world through our own eyes. This guilt, rooted in our existential structure, is a potent source for a sound humility and an attitude of forgiveness toward others. This second form of guilt May calls *Mitwelt*, the world of our relationships with others.

There is a third form of ontological guilt (*Umwelt*) which involves our relation to the cosmos as well as to ourselves and others. It is a guilt over separation, experienced in connection with nature as a whole, and as such, is a more complex and comprehensive aspect of guilt than either of the other two. Ontological guilt, in its three forms, contains several characteristics, says May. First, we all participate in it. All of us have a distorted perception of our fellowman, and fail to fulfill totally our potentialities. Second, ontological guilt does not stem from cultural prohibitions, or from an introjection of cultural mores; its origin is the fact of self-awareness. It does not consist of "we-are-guilty-because-we-violate-parental-prohibitions," but arises out of the fact that we can see ourselves as those who can choose or fail to choose. Third, ontological guilt must not be confused with morbid or neurotic guilt. If we can become aware of ontological guilt and learn to accept it, it is neither morbid nor neurotic. Fourth, ontological guilt does not lead to the formation of symptoms but instead (ideally, at least) leads to humility, a sharpened sensitivity in our interrelationships and an increased creativity in utilizing our own potentialities.

A clear distinction must be made, May reasons, between normal and neurotic guilt.[63] Normal guilt is appropriate

---

[63]May, *Psychology and the Human Dilemma*, pp. 105-08.

to the situation; it is not repressed into unconsciousness, and does not involve symptom formation. It is associated with admitting that what we say always does some violence to absolute truth. Finally, it has a constructive effect in the personality. Normal guilt inheres in our contacts with our fellowman. Our social intercourse is to be open, humble and loving. In our intra-psychic life we are to live out our potentialities and be faithful to our needs, powers and sensitivities. When we are aware that we have betrayed something of significance in our being, we experience guilt.

Neurotic guilt, conversely, is the end result of unconfronted, repressed, normal guilt.[64] The counselor helps us confront our guilt and its implications. While aiding us to free ourselves from neurotic guilt feeling, his positive contribution is to assist us to accept courageously and affirm creatively our normal guilt feelings. May deplores the fact that so often we consider guilt feelings to be unhealthy, for he maintains that a final unity in the human spirit is neither possible nor desirable. Personality is dynamic, not static; creative not vegetative. We do not wish to wipe away conflicts altogether, but instead to transform destructive conflicts into constructive ones.[65]

Guilt feeling, then, is actually a positive, constructive emotion. It is a perception of the discrepancy between what a thing is and what it ought to be, experienced many times a day. It is inescapable in human personality, for it is inseparably connected with freedom, autonomy and moral responsibility. Since we possess creative freedom, we must constantly be glimpsing new possibilities, but with each comes not only a challenge but a feeling of guilt. Guilt feeling inheres in every state of tension in personality; in fact, it is simply a consequence of consciousness. Adam's fall from grace proves that "knowing produces guilt."[66]

However we explain guilt feeling, we must admit that it

[64]*Ibid.*, p. 108.
[65]May, *The Art of Counseling*, pp. 69, 74.
[66]*Ibid.*, pp. 70-73.

proves there is some contradiction in our nature. We are caught between two worlds (in reality, two aspects of the same world) and we must hold within ourselves the tension between the two. Out of this ultimate tension comes our religion. The contradiction in us is proof of the presence of God in human nature. So guilt feeling, far from being something morbid or worthy of shame, is actually proof of our great possibilities and destiny. Any picture of personality which leaves out the aspect of religious tension is incomplete. Healthy individuals make a creative adjustment to God, and a sound religion is indispensable to personality health.[67]

A Christian Perspective

In the previous sections of this chapter the views of theoreticians representing the psychoanalytic, neo-analytic and existentialist positions have been presented. Others, of course, have made significant contributions to our understanding regarding guilt, notably Soren Kierkegaard, the first existentialist, and O. H. Mowrer, a contemporary clinical psychologist and outspoken critic of Freud. In developing a Christian perspective on this critical issue, we will draw upon the ideas of these two men, along with the previously-discussed theoreticians as well as a number of Christian writers.

Our existential condition is one of guilt; we stand guilty before God for deeds consciously committed that have violated our own individual consciences as well as the moral law of God. As the Apostle Paul declares, "None is righteous, no, not one" (Romans 3:10).[68] All of us come under this guilt and condemnation. Moral guilt is not the invention of the Bible or of the Church; it is the universal condition of the human soul.[69]

Guilt feelings, Mavis observes, constitute a heavy burden,

---

[67]*Ibid.*, pp. 73-74.
[68]See also: Psalms 53:3; Genesis 6:5; I Kings 8:46; Proverbs ·20:9.
[69]Paul Tournier, *Guilt and Grace*, trans. by Arthur W. Heathcote J. J. Henry and P. J. Allcock. (New York: Harper and Row, 1962), p. 135.

an intolerable drag on life; they are disintegrating in the sense that they cause us to look backward instead of forward.[70] No single influence has done more to prevent us from finding God and rebuilding our character, or has done more to lower society's moral tone, says Sheen,[71] than the *denial* of personal guilt.

O. H. Mowrer is in agreement with Freud that guilt should be a central consideration in dealing with neurosis, but their viewpoints are in complete opposition. To Mowrer guilt is real while to Freud it is illusory. Guilt, in Mowrer's judgment, is to be faced and dealt with, never swept away and ignored. Instead of being reassured that we are the victims of forces beyond our control (Freud's stance), we must be urged to confess our sins and live in honesty and openness with others.[72]

A therapist must be able to distinguish between false and true guilt. When we experience a sense of guilt, only to be told that the feeling is false, we become distressed and confused. To be taught that there is "no guilt, only shame" does not bring relief, for we do not relieve minds with dictionaries.[73] True guilt is God's judgment through the conscience, and as such is an act of grace. False guilt, conversely, comes about through the judgments of men, and creates intolerable burdens for us to carry.[74]

Three distinct kinds of guilt press for our consideration: psychological, social and spiritual. Rollo May refers to them as *Eigenwelt*, *Mitwelt* and *Umwelt*, respectively.[75] The first arises from forfeiting our own potentialities, the second is related to our fellowmen, and the third is the "separation

---

[70]W. Curry Mavis, *The Psychology of Christian Experience* (Grand Rapids: Zondervan Publishing House, 1963), pp. 26-27.

[71]Fulton J. Sheen, "Morbidity and the Denial of Guilt," in *Morality and Mental Health*, ed. by O. Hobart Mowrer (Chicago: Rand McNally and Company, 1967), p. 232.

[72]O. Hobart Mowrer, *The New Group Therapy*, An Insight Book. (Princeton: D. VanNostrand Company, 1964), p. 144.

[73]Tournier, *Guilt and Grace*, p. 92.

[74]Tweedie, *Logotherapy*, p. 168.

[75]May, Angel and Ellenberger, eds., *Existence*, pp. 54-55.

guilt" pertaining to the cosmos as well as to ourselves and others.

Psychological guilt and anxiety are closely related. Our condition when confronted with the issue of fulfilling our potentialities, either toward ourselves or others, is anxiety. To deny them or fail to fulfill them is to feel guilt. Anxiety would not exist if there were no possiblity whatever. Creating involves demolishing the status quo, giving up old patterns within ourselves and progressively destroying what we have always clung to and bringing into being new, original ways of living. If we do not do this, we are shirking our responsibility toward ourselves.[76]

Anxiety may be distinguished from guilt, however, says Tweedie.[77] Guilt is a manageable phenomenon, localized, and specific; while anxiety is generalized, diffused, unrecognizable and unmanageable. Anxiety is a dread of the future, while guilt is a dread of the past. In the former the wrong decision may *be* made, but in the latter the despair is based upon the fact that the wrong decision has already *been made*.

Tournier[78] aptly describes psychological guilt (*Eigenwelt*) as precisely the failure to dare to be ourselves. It is the fear of the judgments of others that prevents us from being ourselves, from showing our tastes, our desires, our convictions, from developing ourselves and expanding freely in accordance with our own nature.

The second form of guilt, rather than dealing with our "private conscience," is the guilt of our social relationships. Social guilt overwhelms us an infinite number of times every day, declares May.[79] Whenever we pass a cripple begging on the street or a drunkard in the gutter, when by neglect or conscious deed we do harm to another, when we think about war and bloodshed all over the world, or about the ghettos with their tragic poverty, or the inequalities between

[76]Rollo May, *The Meaning of Anxiety* (New York: The Ronald Press, 1950), pp. 38-39.

[77]Tweedie, *Christian and the Couch*, p. 101.

[78]Tournier, *Guilt and Grace*, p. 17.

[79]May, *The Art of Counseling*, pp. 70-71.

races, nationalities and classes in our educational, economic and social structures — in short, whenever we have a feeling that conditions ought to be different from the way they are, we experience social guilt.

The third category of guilt, the spiritual, is as real as happiness or love; it operates in us because conscience and God exist. Christianity provides a decisive answer to the problem of spiritual guilt.

Our basic predicament is estrangement from God, as Mavis[80] analyzes it, which causes, in turn, an estrangement from our essential being and our fellowman. Guilt has brought about this estrangement; we feel estranged from God because we have sinned against Him. We feel restive over our sense of estrangement, for we wish to be related to both our Creator and to our fellowman. We have no greater personal need than relief from this sense of isolation and estrangement.

Weatherhead specifies two difficult roads we may take in response to a sense of guilt.[81] We take the first road, *depression*, if we consciously accept the fact of guilt and are spiritually sensitive and introspective. We may be overcome with despair, and cry with St. Paul, "Wretched man that I am! Who will deliver me from this body of death?" (Romans 7:24). Sorrow for sin can lead us to confession. If, on the other hand, we take the road of *repression* and pretend the guilt is not there or banish it into the unconscious, it may, from those inaccessible depths, initiate a mental distress or physical illness difficult for our physician either to understand or cure.

According to whether guilt is repressed or recognized, it sets in motion one of two opposing processes; if repressed, it may be expected to lead to anger, rebellion, fear, anxiety, a deadening of conscience, an increasing inability to recognize our faults, and a growing ascendance of aggressive tenden-

---

[80]Mavis, *The Psychology of Christian Experience*, pp. 49-50.
[81]Leslie D. Weatherhead, *Psychology, Religion and Healing* (New York: Abingdon-Cokesbury Press, 1951), pp. 323-24.

cies. But if it is consciously recognized, it may lead to repentance, to peace and security as a result of divine pardon,
and thus to a progressive refinement of conscience. It is
not guilt which is the obstacle to grace but the repression of
guilt, which takes the forms of self-justification, genuine self-
righteousness and smugness. Repression is an ageless and universal reaction, Tournier avows, dating back to Adam and
Eve in the garden.[82]

With depression, repression and suppression providing the
unattractive alternatives, we look for yet another way to
confront our overwhelming load of guilt. Such an alternative, which is both psychologically and spiritually sound, is
repentance. Repentance is essential for the restoration of
the health of the mind and soul and has vast implications
even for the health of the body. The prime source of our
guilt lies in a broken relationship with God and our fellowman, through the separating element of sin. We may be
absolved of that guilt by entering into a vital relationship
with God, that of sonship, through faith in the person and
work of Jesus Christ. We enter it by turning from the sins
of our life, which are the root cause of our anxiety and guilt,
to Christ in repentance and faith, thus receiving assurance of
forgiveness and at-one-ment.

The power of sin in our lives is broken as we appropriate
by faith the results of the vicarious suffering and death of
Christ. His work there completely destroyed the objective
power of evil. The death of the God-Man provides the
bridge over which we can approach God in confidence for
the absolution of our sins. Believing in the efficacy of His
blood to cleanse from sin and believing that He died for the
sins of all, and, more personally, for our *own* sins, we accept by faith the free gift of His salvation. In taking such a
step we are acknowledging that there is no other way of
atonement — that there is "no other name given among men
by which we must be saved" (Acts 4:12) — that the cross
upon which the Saviour died is the end of the road to despair and the beginning of the road to life. The ingredients

---

[82]Tournier, *Guilt and Grace*, p. 137.

of freedom from guilt arising from sin, then, are faith in Christ's atoning work at Calvary, and repentance, which involves turning away from all conscious sin.

The human need for confession and repentance, Jung argues,[83] is written into the very nature of the universe. It is only with the aid of repentance that we can throw ourselves "into the arms of humanity, at last freed from the burden of moral exile." Lacking this, an impenetrable wall prevents us from feeling a part of the human race.

Weatherhead contends[84] that many of us, while intellectually subscribing to the fact of God's forgiveness, have never felt forgiven, because our confession has not gone deep enough. He recommends a written confession, even if we tear it up afterwards, for writing it out has the value of, as William James expresses it, "exteriorising our rottenness."[85] God's forgiveness is the most powerful therapeutic idea in the world. If we truly believe that God has forgiven us, the burden of guilt and the fear behind it disappear. Many scriptural promises support this contention. Our sin will be remembered no more (Jeremiah 31:34); it is behind God's back (Isaiah 38:17); it is removed from the sinner "as far as the east is from the west" (Psalm 103:12). When we hear an authoritative voice, saying the words, "Thy sins are forgiven thee," we speedily take up our beds and walk.

There is frequently more to the process of freedom from guilt than confession to God. Because sin is so frequently expressed in acts against our fellows, restitution, while difficult to do, is necessary for total restoration. "Leave your gift there before the altar and go; first be reconciled to your brother, and then come and offer your gift" (Matthew 5:24).

Exteriorization and reparation, then, facilitate our acceptance of forgiveness. The relating and unburdening of our own guilt to the "significant others," and thus knowing the

[83]Jung, *Modern Man in Search of a Soul*, p. 41.
[84]Weatherhead, *Psychology, Religion and Healing*, pp. 332-34, 448-49.
[85]William James, *The Varieties of Religious Experience* (London: Longmans, Green, and Company, 1911), p. 462.

healing power of reconciliation, is the balm for a world which
has all but lost its capacity for openness and humility.[86] Radical openness with "significant others" in our lives not only is
a most effective means of "treatment," but also is a strong pre-
ventive of difficulty. We cannot know ourselves without disclosing ourselves to another. Such disclosure is the antithesis
of repression and self-alienation.[87]

Some of us are unable to forgive ourselves for our past
sins and dwell morbidly upon them, even though God has
forgiven us. We foster within ourselves a need for self-pun-
ishment, as if we could somehow atone for our sins by our
own suffering. Mowrer seems to justify this kind of thinking,
maintaining that we should "pay for our sins by long and intense suffering, perhaps even institutionalization." Confession
is to be as "broad as the sin itself" and when we have "paid
our debt to society" we will be free.[88] This is a legalistic
form of reasoning. To refuse to forgive ourselves is not only
spiritually damaging; it displays a distrust of God's work in
our lives, a misconception of the nature of God, as well as a
lack of faith. Restitution, where practicable and in response
to God's leadings, enhances our Christian witness and experience, but a morbid self-hating attitude may do inestimable
damage to our own psyche as well as to the cause of Christ.

Scripture and other great literature, along with experience,
will support the contention that we are accountable to God
for our thought life as well as our actions. Jesus' teachings,
in His Sermon on the Mount and elsewhere, uphold the contention that the ultimate consideration is the motive behind
the action, rather than the action itself. Dostoevsky's classic,
The Brothers Karamazov, where Ivan's insanity comes as a
direct result of the wish for his father's death, illustrates this

---

[86]Erwin A. Gaede, "The Priesthood of Sinners" in *Morality and Mental Health*, ed. by O. Hobart Mowrer (Chicago: Rand McNally and Company, 1967), p. 341.

[87]Mowrer, *The New Group Therapy*, pp. 90, 230, 236.

[88]O. Hobart Mowrer, *Crisis in Psychiatry and Religion*, An In-sight Book. (Princeton, New Jersey: D. VanNostrand Company, 1961), pp. 99-101.

important point. Solomon's wise words underscore it: "As he thinketh in his heart, so is he" (Proverbs 23:7, KJV).

Throwing a relentless beam upon the secret depths of human personality, Christ locates guilt, not in a legalism that focuses on outward deeds, but in our hearts: "Go, sell what you possess," He tells the rich, self-righteous young ruler (Matthew 19:21), and instructs the Pharisees: "For out of the heart come evil thoughts. . . . (Matthew 15:19-20).

The Sermon on the Mount, then, is not a recipe for freedom from guilt by meritorious conduct. On the contrary, it is the shattering word that convicts us of murder when we have done no killing, adultery when we have not committed the act, or hatred when we have boasted of our love. It is the opposite, actually, of a moral code. Christ, in opposing a primitive taboo moralism, proclaims that we are all equally sinful despite our moral efforts, and that we find forgiveness, not by showing off our vaunted impeccability, but by confessing our guilt and repenting of our sins.[89]

The *Faith at Work* movement serves as an example of a group who is attempting to take personal guilt seriously and is making active use of confession and restitution in an attempt to meet needs and to restore individuals to a sense of community. Mowrer[90] reports observing six hundred people at one of their conferences engaged in a form of interaction and community life describable as a "reasonable and living facsimile of the Apostolic Church." The central theme in the testimonies of participants is that, having been in sin and misery, they are rediscovering, as a result of a new policy of openness and restitution, a sense of at-one-ment with others and God, and are experiencing, as a result, serenity and joy.

While heartily endorsing the principles being employed by this group in their efforts to maintain relationship and community with God and others, we would not want to leave the impression that any of us ever quite "arrives" in this matter of spiritual attainment. Guilt feelings will be perpetuated in our relationships with ourselves, as we sense our own possi-

[89]Tournier, *Guilt and Grace*, pp. 121-22.
[90]Mowrer, *The New Group Therapy*, pp. 20-21.

bilities, gaps and inadequacies. This is no less true in our relationships with others, for we cannot possibly right all the wrongs of the world. A constantly increasing sense of social obligation is an integral part of the life of the Christian. Life represents an infinite number of possibilities, with an obligation to fulfill them. Thus there never can be fulfillment.

The spiritual life is a process, not a state, and while we narrow the gap some disparity will always remain. Life without such a gap would be life without a challenge. Guilt feeling is the perception of a gap, by definition. Our inner being remains a scene of conflict, for we are not yet perfected in love. The more mature we become in our outlook the more we realize our imperfect condition.[91]

In our conflict we experience, according to Tournier,[92] both guilt and grace simultaneously.

> This can be seen in history; for believers who are most desperate about themselves are the ones who express most forcefully their confidence in grace. . . . To imagine that after conversion one is sheltered from . . . guilt is to beguile oneself with a dangerous illusion. . . .
>
> What grace removes is not guilt, but condemnation. St. Paul is quite clear: "There is therefore now no condemnation".

To summarize, if we set as our spiritual goal simply to return to a normal state where guilt feelings do not have a debilitating effect upon us we set a pathetically low level of aspiration for ourselves. Handling guilt feelings can be a creative experience, which drives us to our knees in dependence upon God for strength and power to overcome our circumstances and temptations, vision to glimpse new possibilities and courage to reach for them. We are aware that we may fail and that the gap may be widened rather than narrowed. But as growing Christians we are willing to take the risk.

Our life is to be lived in the dynamic tension between the possibility of His coming and the responsibility for being good

---

[91]May, *The Art of Counseling*, pp. 72, 222-23.
[92]Tournier, *Guilt and Grace*, pp. 159-60.

stewards over our lives. We must keep our spiritual books up to date. This entails frequent confession to God about our weaknesses, proneness toward wandering, evil thinking and speaking, etc. It also involves our willingness to admit our wrongs toward others, any bad spirit, hasty or critical word expressed, neglected opportunity to help, etc.

But while we are introspective, our spirituality is balanced by action. We are admonished: "Attempt great things for God; expect great things from God." We must not view our lives as isolated entities needing constant defending against the inroads of wickedness. Rather, we are heirs of God and joint-heirs with His Son, Jesus Christ — made in His image, extensions of His personality. Such a realization should help us to face life confidently and witness spontaneously of His grace. Athletic coaches and militarists are in essential agreement that a good offense is the best defense. So it is in Christian living. To be about the Master's business, drawing upon Him for courage and strength, is to mount an offensive that can overcome the potentially debilitating effects of guilt. As we are armed with the assurance that prostrating ourselves at the foot of Calvary's cross means we can arise assured of Christ's forgiveness and filled with His power and love, feelings of anxiety and guilt will be forced to retreat.

Guilt, then, is not overcome by constant, fearful introspection, but by uninhibited and total investment in the Kingdom of God. Such an investment provides a hedge against being overtaken by feelings of guilt and anxiety, and provides the motivation that makes life intensely worthwhile. It is to this important concept that we turn now.

Discussion Questions

1. Can we deal effectively with our guilt by will power?
2. Why is it so important that we deal effectively with guilt?
3. What *positive* effects has guilt feeling had in your life?
4. Is there a difference between confession and repentance?
5. Why are so many Christians unable to forgive themselves?
6. What advantages and disadvantages are there to discussing in a group our mutual failures and shortcomings?

III

The Springs of Motivation

INTRODUCTION

MOTIVATION HAS BEEN STUDIED with intense interest from earliest times. Ancient philosophers, lacking modern-day understanding and insight, were attempting to deal with what appeared to them to be supernatural forces. Even as recently as the early twentieth century, Henri Bergson, the French philosopher, was propounding the idea of "elan vital" (creative force) as a universal phenomenon within us all. Scientifically-oriented psychologists have reacted against such ideas, and the study of motivation tended to fall into disrepute. Boring's *History of Experimental Psychology*, published in 1929, in fact, contains no reference to motivation. More recently, however, motivation, i.e., how behavior is aroused, directed, sustained and/or controlled, has gained an academic respectability and currently is one of the more important concepts in the field.[1]

Psychologists, in general, have handled the issue of motivation badly. For one thing, we have been far too pessimistic regarding ourselves and our potentialities for change and greatness. A major reason for this is that as psychologists and psychiatrists we have spent nearly all of our time dealing with the seriously disturbed people among us, represented by the "5 per cent." Our writings reflect an over-concern with

---

[1]Ruch, *Psychology and Life*, 7th ed., p. 375.

the abnormal, with the result that the extent to which our personalities can unfold toward self-fulfillment has received little attention. Psychology would be a vastly different field today if those of us within it would have concentrated 95 per cent of our time and thinking on the 95 per cent who may be classified as *well*.

Another grave error has been to focus upon only one propriate function as the explanation of motivation. Thus, Nietzscheans have fixed upon the lust for power (or self-assertion), Thomists upon the rational function, Freudians upon the libido, etc. The truth is that all functions have a place, and to depict motivation as dependent upon any one function to the exclusion of others is to portray a one-sided picture of true personality growth.[2]

A third factor is that most "favored" theories of motivation have in common the basic assumption that all behavior tends toward equilibrium and the elimination of states of excitation. All excitability, striving and tension have their source in the disturbance of organic equilibrium. The more severe the disturbance the greater becomes the urgency to reduce the tension. Some of these theories place emphasis upon the negative result (avoidance of pain or discomfort), others on the positive (the attainment of pleasurable consequences). For Freud, the instincts all strive toward pleasure. Fundamentally, Freudian and behavioristic models are alike, as are all other theories holding quiescence, complacency, or pleasure to be the goals of action. While our drives do represent urgent demands for tension-reduction, this is only half of the problem. While we want stability, we also want variety, and it is only through risk-taking and variation that growth can occur.[3]

Knowing why people behave as they do is of interest to everyone whose success depends on dealing with others. We all tend to make conscious (or unconscious) appraisals of the

---

[2]Gordon W. Allport, *Becoming: Basic Considerations for a Psychology of Personality* (New Haven: Yale University Press, 1955), p. 57.

[3]*Ibid.*, p. 65.

needs, interests, values and emotions that motivate the behavior of others. It is not surprising, then, that classifications
of motivational dispositions abound in the literature. This is
consistent with the tendency within any science to begin by
sorting out its objects of investigation. Even though it may
abandon these earlier sortings, the field has been aided in de-
fining its subject matter. Hilgard,[4] suggests that psychology
is in this state presently, and that no list has been agreed upon
as containing all of the appropriate categories. Four representative lists are the "four wishes" by W. I. Thomas,[5] H. A.
Murray's list of 12 viscerogenic (physiological) needs and 28
psychogenic needs,[6] A. H. Maslow's hierarchy of needs[7] and
Erich Fromm's five human needs.[8] The latter two will be
discussed later in this chapter. To observe the variety of lists,
and the length and scope of Murray's concept of needs, may
help us become apprised of the enormity of the task of com-
pleting a theory of human motivation. En route to a Christian
viewpoint of motivation, we recognize the importance of fa-
miliarizing ourselves with psychoanalytic, neo-analytic, exis-
tentialistic, behavioristic and humanistic concepts, and it is to
this task we apply ourselves now.

THE VIEW OF THE PSYCHOANALYST

Sigmund Freud

Freudian psychoanalysis has made three significant and
permanent contributions, says Horney: first, that psychic processes are strictly determined; i.e., all of our acts have an-
tecedents, largely traceable; that our actions and feelings may
be determined by unconscious motivations; and that those mo-

---

[4]Ernest R. Hilgard and Richard C. Atkinson, *Introduction to Psychology* (4th ed., New York: Harcourt, Brace and World, 1967),
pp. 142-43.
[5]W. I. Thomas, *The Unadjusted Girl* (Boston: Little, Brown,
1923).
[6]Henry A. Murray, et. al., *Explorations in Personality* (New York:
Oxford University Press, 1938).
[7]Maslow, *Motivation and Personality*, pp. 80-106.
[8]Fromm, *The Sane Society*, pp. 27-66.

tivations driving us are emotional forces, understood only in a context of conflict, needs, frustrations and feelings.[9] While many have had, over the centuries, a vague awareness of the fact that the unconscious assumes certain controls over our conduct, Freud is credited, and rightly so, with discovering the powerful role of unconscious motives in human behavior. He cites three forms of behavior through which unconscious motives are expressed: 1) dreams; 2) unconscious mannerisms and slips of speech; and 3) symptoms of illness, especially neurotic illness.[10]

According to Freud, all three parts of our mind (superego, ego and id) contribute to the direction of our lives. The superego is the internal voice of our parents and society. Too much tension between the demands of the superego and ego produces a sense of guilt. The more highly developed our ego becomes, the greater our control over our instincts. Our ego develops gradually as self-esteem, pride and respect for others increase. Our ego is the battleground for the contest waged between our passionate id and our strict conscience. A strong ego can properly direct our primitive instincts in a spontaneous, imaginative and constructive way. If our id is held down too harshly and if we live by too strict a moral code so that we suffer an overwhelming sense of guilt, we will be unhappy. On the other hand, if we lack sufficient superego, abandoning ourselves to every destructive impulse, we end up in the same unhappy state. Only when there is harmony between id, ego and superego can we live peacefully with ourselves and those we love.[11]

We are driven by two main instincts, the aggressive, self-protective or hate instinct, which allows us to keep alive in the midst of danger, and the sexual or love instinct, which insures the perpetuation of the species. Life would be simple if it were not for the conflict between our id and our superego. When we deny an instinct direct gratification, it will at-

---

[9]Horney, *New Ways in Psychoanalysis*, pp. 18; 22-23.
[10]Hilgard and Atkinson, *Introduction to Psychology*, p. 149.
[11]Lucy Freeman, *Why People Act That Way* (New York: Thomas Crowell, 1965), pp. 61-64.

tempt to escape in one way or another. If it finds an approved form of expression, we experience satisfaction and a rise in self-respect, but if it does not, we are likely to repress it and suffer the grievous effects of repression.[12]

The pleasure principle governs our life at birth. What brings pleasure we love; what brings displeasure we hate. As we grow, we learn to replace, in large part, the pleasure principle with the reality principle. We do not give up pleasure entirely, but we settle for a substitute, or for a partial gratification or postponement of immediate gratification. Our parents inevitably and frequently frustrate us, and we hate them for it. The more we are frustrated the greater our hatred, and, in turn, the greater our guilt over our hatred. We must learn to accept frustration or become unhappy adults, unable to live comfortably with anyone. In infancy, we are primarily concerned with ourselves, our needs and our desires. Most of us give up a certain amount of this narcissism (self-love) in childhood, even though it is painful and goes contrary to nature, for one important reason: to obtain the love of our parents, without which we know we cannot survive.[13]

For mature persons there is more pleasure in controlling instincts than indulging them. This pleasure springs from learning how to direct our aggressive and sexual feelings. Without such sublimation we would be at the complete mercy of our impulses. Successful sublimation of aggressive and sexual instincts is of prime importance in our civilization. Most of us are able to handle these in ways that offer substitute gratifications, e.g., through sports, work, art, hobbies, etc. Freud does not say that *all* aggressive and sexual energy should be sublimated. A certain amount of aggression is needed for the sex act and for survival, but over and above this minimum, we are expected to sublimate.[14]

In dealing with our frustrations, however, we do not or cannot always sublimate. Many times we repress our urges

---

[12]*Ibid.*, pp. 66-68.
[13]*Ibid.*, pp. 68-70.
[14]*Ibid.*, pp. 70-71, 156, 166-69.

from consciousness. Freud distinguishes two kinds of unconsciousness: one is latent, but capable of coming to consciousness (pre-conscious), and the other, the true unconscious, is repressed and ordinarily incapable of becoming conscious. He argues that the concept of mind should include processes which are unconscious, i.e., repressed, along with the conscious and pre-conscious. He offers many "proofs" of its existence. Conscious acts remain disconnected and unintelligible if we hold to the claim that all mental acts performed have to be consciously experienced. While he does not state that the unconscious mind is created solely by repression, he does insist that repression is a potent source of unconscious energies and a prime cause of psychopathology. An idea banished from consciousness frequently continues in its striving for recognition and expression, and this striving constitutes the principal basis of anxiety and ensuing symptom formation. The mental processes most likely to undergo repression are the instinctual forces of sexuality and hostility and this repression ordinarily occurs when the ego, under the sway of the superego, rejects and condemns these impulses. Resolving a conflict between an instinct and a moral scruple by repression demands a constant expenditure of energy, and is unsatisfactory as well as debilitating.

Therapy aims to undo repressions that have accumulated, thus permitting our sexual and hostile impulses to find freer, less encumbered routes to gratification.[15] The primary technique used in psychoanalytic therapy is free association, by which we bring to consciousness our repressed conflicts, as the therapist encourages the free flow of ideas, which he then interprets. By tracing impulses back to their roots in the past, the present emotional overreaction to them can be minimized. On the strength of this information we are helped to achieve an appropriate balance between the forces of ego, superego and id, so that constructive actions will be facilitated.[16]

---

[15]Mowrer, *Crisis in Psychiatry and Religion*, pp. 18-20.
[16]Arnold and Gasson, *The Human Person*, p. 506.

Alfred Adler

In opposition to Freud's concept of motivation, Adler sees the dynamic force in the individual as a striving for superiority or power. This striving is similar to, although not identical with, the "will to power" theories of Nietzsche and Schopenhauer. Adler's will is more a will to prestige than power. There is an urge within our ego to gain superiority over our fellows and attain a position of security which cannot be threatened. Inferiority feeling is a universal phenomenon. It develops in infancy, as we see adults walking, lifting things and exerting power which we lack. It also has roots in the real inferiority of our primitive ancestors as they strove with the animals. The development of civilization is to be understood as the history of our strivings to overcome inferiority.[17]

In early childhood we have strong feelings of inferiority shown by our wish to exclude stronger children and play with weaker ones whom we can dominate. This striving never ceases. Life is the attainment of a goal and it is the striving for superiority which sets the process in motion toward the attainment of that goal.[18]

Our striving receives its specific direction from an *individually unique* goal or self-ideal. Even as children there is no such thing as an absolutely fixed and right way for us to respond. We strive in our own individual ways toward a better style of life, making our own mistakes and "approximations to success."[19]

Our style of life extends into the realms of emotional and physical development. To illustrate: if our individual life style makes a significant place for courage, our feelings and characteristic reactions grow in that direction to the point necessary to implement that goal. As a result, the body will be stronger, the muscles will be more firmly toned, the posture will be more erect. The features and expressions —

---

[17]May, *The Art of Counseling*, pp. 63-64.
[18]Alfred Adler, *The Science of Living* (New York: Garden City Publishing Company, 1929), pp. 74, 79-80.
[19]*Ibid.*, pp. 65, 99-100.

even the "conformation of the skull" — reflect our self-ideal.[20]

In the spiritual realm this striving may be seen as an instinct toward perfection. Though we cannot be like the eternally complete, all-loving and all-powerful God, His call nevertheless directs us toward perfection, toward overcoming the feelings of lowliness and transitoriness of our existence here below. We are endowed with the ability to participate in our own uplift, elevation, perfection and completion.[21]

Adler deals with the human strivings toward self-establishment and achievement. We strive with the intention of achieving dominance over things and individuals, a striving that is necessary for self-actuation. What particular possessions or achievements we strive for depend upon our interests; thus we develop our individual "life-style." The core of this self-styling is the striving for self-actuation, or excellence. It becomes excessive and develops into a striving for superiority only when the tendency is allowed free play instead of being subordinated to a rational goal, the self-ideal, as it ought to be.[22]

An exaggerated inferiority feeling may be expected to lead to neurotic behavior, for it gives the ego an abnormally strong striving for power. Behind cases of driving ambition there lurks a deep, though possibly unconscious, inferiority feeling. In our strivings for prestige, to lower others is equivalent to raising ourselves. This explains why we derive pleasure from gossiping. The normal ambition for power is to be differentiated from the neurotic. Normal striving proceeds from strength and may or may not be antisocial; neurotic ambition proceeds from weakness and insecurity, and derives its pleasure from debasing and dominating others.[23]

[20]Alfred Adler, *What Life Should Mean to You* (New York: Capricorn Books, 1958), pp. 31, 43.

[21]Heinz L. and Rowena R. Ansbacher, *The Individual Psychology of Alfred Adler*, A Basic Book. (New York: Basic Books, 1956), pp. 106-07.

[22]Arnold and Gasson, *The Human Person*, p. 507.

[23]*Ibid.*, pp. 65-66.

Any analysis of individual life styles must be made in a social context, Adler argues.[24] The main problems in life demand human cooperation for their solution. Childhood socialization experiences, therefore, are of major significance. The school as well as the home assumes tremendous importance in developing our social interest and training us to take responsible places in society.

Adler's concepts have had considerable impact upon later motivational theorists, especially Fromm and Rank. The existentialist school of psychotherapy has adopted many of Adler's teachings while repudiating many of their analytic implications.[25]

Carl Jung

Jung, the great Swiss psychoanalyst, has contributed substantially to motivational theory. He has created a vague and tenuous "collective unconscious" to take the place of Freud's psychoanalytic unconscious. In this "collective unconscious" he has posited archetypes. He has developed the idea of introvert and extrovert. Perhaps of greatest significance is his concept of "individuation" or the realization of self through the finding of God. Each of these ideas is worthy of separate consideration.

Jung argues that we have both a personal and collective unconscious.[26] If only the personal unconscious exists, when successful analysis takes place and repressed materials are brought to the surface, the unconscious will be emptied and rendered unable to manufacture fantasies and dreams. But it obviously continues to perform this function. The collective unconscious seems not to be a person, but more like a flowing stream of images and figures which drift into unconsciousness in our dreams and in certain abnormal states of mind, and thus contains a potential wisdom.

---

[24]Adler, *The Science of Living*, pp. 199, 214.
[25]Jan Ehrenwald, *From Medicine Man to Freud*, A Dell Book. (New York: Dell, 1956), pp. 346-48.
[26]Weatherhead, *Psychology, Religion and Healing*, p. 278.

During times of strain, we revert to primordial ways of
thinking and acting and are attracted to myths, legends, fa-
bles, witchcraft, proverbs and the like, which have existed in
the literature of all races. Their appeal lies in the fact that
they express a truth or an experience which we recognize in
our collective unconscious. These myths, etc., are a vast, inherited reservoir of racial memories and experiences. They
have never been put into language, for they are deeper than
thought. They constitute material once conscious and later
repressed as well as material which never has been and prob-
ably never will be conscious. There seem to be some psychi-
cal qualities, such as instinctive activities, which have nothing
to do with us as individuals yet have a repetitiveness which
suggests that they come from a deeper stratum than any individual mind.[27]

These deeper levels constitute a certain psychic disposition
shaped by the forces of heredity. They include our hopes,
fears, images, and every variety of psychic content. Out of
this great reservoir come the fantasies which become the
great art of mankind, the creative ideas which are the embryos
of philosophies, and the insights which are developed into
religions. They are the inner urges that give content to our
living.[28]

Personality develops according to the laws laid down in
the unconscious; the conscious has to step aside and let the
unconscious live through the conscious. No objective goal,
then, can serve as the focus for our striving; we are developing, by an evolutionary force, toward autarchy. Jung, in therapy, explores the personal and collective unconscious to help
us toward autarchic growth, and toward increasing our self-
knowledge, thus leading to more effective self-determination.[29]

Dispositions arising from the collective unconscious, sometimes called "primordial ideas" or "collective images," Jung

[27]*Ibid.*, pp. 278-79, 286.
[28]May, *The Art of Counseling*, p. 183.
[29]Arnold and Gasson, *The Human Person*, p. 511.

calls "archetypes," a term borrowed from St. Augustine.
We find religion and God in the deepest levels of our collective unconscious, for the idea of God is an archetype.[30] The
archetypes are "inherited potentialities of human imagination." They are "systems of preparedness" as well as images and emotions. They are not inherited ideas, but inherited
possibilities of ideas, inherent within the structure of the
brain. Our dreams, drawings and paintings give a useful clue
about our unconscious attitudes, for such reflections of our
personality spring from and satisfy basic needs. Through
them, we bring to expression that part of the psyche which
reaches back into the primitive past and reconciles it with
present-day consciousness.[31]

"Finding religion" consists of exploring these deep levels of
the unconscious and assimilating them into our conscious living. To do so is to become reconciled to ourselves and thus
reconciled to adverse circumstances and events. The archetypes serve as our spiritual guides which supplant the totally
inadequate ego.[32]

One of Jung's most important claims[33] is that we are either
extroverts or introverts, depending upon our physical makeup.
To be normal is to effect a balance between the two; but
because of outer circumstances and the pull of unconscious
and subjective factors, most of us react characteristically one
way or the other. It is this habitual reaction that makes us
either an extrovert or an introvert. Personality involves the
functions of thinking, feeling, sensation and intuition. If one
prevails, a corresponding personality type results; e.g., the
extrovert is dominated by reverie, and motivated by the
will to power. The libido is, in this scheme, the total life energy moving in the extrovert toward outward objects and
in the introvert toward subjective ideas, interests and aims.

---

[30]May, *The Art of Counseling*, p. 217.
[31]Weatherhead, *Psychology, Religion and Healing*, pp. 279-80.
[32]Jung, *Modern Man in Search of a Soul*, pp. 279-80.
[33]Weatherhead, *Psychology, Religion and Healing*, pp. 282-84.

To divide society into introverts and extroverts, Jung concedes in his later years, fails to allow for dissimilarities between individuals. While many obviously fall into these classes, others are "ambiverts."[34] It is only fair to say that throughout his writings generally Jung emphasizes individuality, perhaps as much as any other leading Freudian thinker.

Jung's ideal type is the foursquare personality.[35] Thinking, feeling, sensation and intuition are all on the same level; none is subordinated and no integration is needed. In practice, however, we have our preference for one of these functions, and the others are correspondingly neglected. Individuation consists of developing all four functions equally, drawing upon the wisdom of the unconscious to provide a balance for the conscious. In this way we are made whole, individuated, effectively utilizing both our conscious and unconscious resources.

What Jung calls individuation is an experience resembling spiritual conversion.[36] It marks the end of our search for the right road, but not the end of our spiritual journey. It is the wise setting of our house of personality in order, but it is a task at which we must work the rest of our lives.

The basic motivation behind human behavior is to find ultimate meaning in the life process. To accomplish this requires faith, hope, love and insight,[37] and demands self-discipline of both character and intellect. Individuation is the process by which we become fully autonomous. Though there seems to be some room for a striving for perfection, the striving that really counts is unconscious and complementary to conscious activity because we cannot escape our natural bent. If we err and miss the goal, it is because we lack awareness of the unconscious processes which would point the way when conscious deliberation fails. Evolution will eventuate in our complete individuation. At the current stage of the

---

[34] Jung, *Modern Man*, p. 100.
[35] Arnold and Gasson, *The Human Person*, p. 510.
[36] Weatherhead, *Psychology, Religion and Healing*, p. 287.
[37] May, *The Art of Counseling*, p. 214.

evolutionary process, however, this level has been reached by only a few individuals.[38]

Otto Rank

Rank's major contribution to motivation theory centers around his concept of will. Its prototype is the Freudian ego. The will itself arises as a resistance to compulsion — either compulsion from the outside in the form of parental commands or from the inside in the form of the demands of the instincts. In either case, active willing is a resistance to compulsions.[39] The therapist focuses his attention upon our will. Resistance, as such, is not to be overcome, but encouraged and strengthened as constructive striving toward independence. Creative expression becomes the goal of treatment.[40] By affirming our will creatively or spiritually, we change our inevitable guilt into "ethical ideal formation," and are spurred on to higher realms of self-development.[41]

Rank regards will, then, as basically positive, resulting in the organization and integration of the self. The self utilizes and, at the same time, inhibits and controls the drives. When this positive action force is added to the inner workings of the system, we have both motive force and direction.[42] We enhance our own personality by creative willing, and neurosis is due precisely to the fact that we cannot will constructively. Neurotics are frequently those who possess unusual creative potentialities, but are unable to adjust personality tensions so as to bring these powers into effective expression.[43]

The task of the therapist is not to act as will for us, which we would like, but to function as counter-will in such a way that our will is strengthened. What we need is the positive ex-

---

[38] Arnold and Gasson, *The Human Person*, p. 554.
[39] *Ibid.*, p. 160.
[40] Lucy Freeman and Marvin Small, *The Story of Psychoanalysis*, A Pocket Book. (New York: Pocket Books, 1960), p. 137.
[41] Rank, *Will Therapy*, p. 242.
[42] Arnold and Gasson, *The Human Person*, p. 159.
[43] May, *The Art of Counseling*, pp. 52, 231.

pression of our will without any inhibiting guilt feeling, a goal which is attained as we "overcome" the therapist and "rule over" the analytic experience. Constructive therapy, then, attempts to transform negative will expression (counter-will) into positive and ultimately creative expressions. Its aim is to free us to be able to accept ourselves as we are. Such a goal stands in contrast to the goals of education and analytic therapy, which Rank asserts are to make of us good citizens who accept our lot without contradiction and without a will of our own.[44]

How external forces are overcome through the freedom of the will is explained by Rank:[45]

> In the perceptual sphere of emotional life the ego modifies the instincts . . . into definite interests or desires whose carrying over into deed or work . . . depends on the spiritual forms . . . created from the individual's ego-ideal formation. This is the schema of a constructive will psychology, in the center of which we place the conscious ego. . . .
> Consciousness, which primarily had been only an expression and tool of the will, soon became a self dependent power, which can not only support and strengthen the will by rationalization, but also is able to repress it through denial. On the other hand, the will which up to then had been only executive now becomes creative, but at first only negatively so, that is, in the form of a denial. The next step serves to justify and maintain this denial and leads to the positive creation of that which should be, that is, to that which is as the ego wills it in terms of its own ideal formation.

Rank identifies two forces in the concept of the conflict of will.[46] The force which we experience in impact with the outside world is our conscious will. The other force is sexuality, which is a stronger power than all external authorities combined. This "generic sexual compulsion," when com-

---

[44]Rank, *Will Therapy*, pp. 16-19, 228.
[45]*Ibid.*, pp. 233, 235.
[46]*Ibid.*, pp. 257-58.

pletely aroused, is so overpowering that we soon begin to de-
fend ourselves against its domination, simply because it is a
domination and we object to being ruled by a strange will.

Freud contends that sexuality is the strongest motivator,
while Rank insists that the will can control it to a great degree. The problem is solved by Rank's mature thinking: neither is adequate, but a third force *is* — namely, the "will to
immortality." The will to immortality, similar to Jung's
"self," is the "autonomous organizing force" within us which
is the creative expression of the total personality, the essence
of our individuality, and the force through which our potentialities are expressed and fulfilled in the world. It expresses all of our unconscious potentialities, our latent creativity and the irrational urges in the depths of our beings.[47]
As the uniting, balancing force between impulses and inhibitions, it is the decisive psychological factor in human behavior.[48]

Rank pleads for an ideology in our modern age capable of
strengthening our will in a creative way.[49] We need a point
of view through which we can experience our immortality
in a believable and livable form, as an enduring and produc-
tive connection to life. Such an ideology must be capable of
drawing forth our latent "genius" and inspiring a new "collective vitality" in our tired civilization. Psychology cannot
carry out this role; we have to go *beyond psychology* to
solve problems related to our deepest nature. We do not act
only upon the rational guidance of our ego, nor are we driven
blindly by the mere elemental forces of our instincts. We
must embrace a world view based on the conception of the
supernatural. We can overcome death by faith. Whichever
method we choose to achieve immortality, it will embody the
assertion of individual will counter to the fixed patterns of
the culture. By creating something that alters the will of
the community we establish the uniqueness of our will and

[47]Progoff, *Death and Rebirth*, pp. 206-07.
[48]Rank, *Beyond Psychology*, p. 50.
[49]Progoff, *Death and Rebirth*, pp. 227-28, 230-32, 265.

thereby gain our immortality. This is the essence of the will to immortality. The task of the new psychology (if psychology lives) is to bring us into contact with the sustaining and creative forces of life beyond our present intellectual doctrines and to make these forces available and verifiable within us.

The motivational force to which Rank points is "life in Christ," which provides us with "real identity." To identify ourselves with Him is to be (as He is) alive and risen from the dead, no longer anxious about an indefinite future. This life, available to all, is a life of faith, not insight, accomplished through love — the kind of love Paul describes in I Corinthians 13. Love, in the sense Rank uses it here, is infinitely more than "sublimated sex"; it is the positive affirmation of the will in surrender to something greater than the "self."[50] Both Christ and Paul are considered by Rank as "highly creative personalities." By replacing outworn values with new life forces, they have provided the impetus and example whereby we in turn likewise may be liberated.

THE VIEW OF A NEO-ANALYST

Erich Fromm

Fromm's motivational theory is rooted in an analysis of human needs.[51] These needs stem from the condition of our existence. All of us strive for the satisfaction of needs which are specifically human, needs which transcend our physiological drives.

The first of the five is relatedness. We are aware of our loneliness, powerlessness and ignorance. To unite with other living beings is imperative. There is but one passion which satisfies our need to unite ourselves with our world, and that is love. Love is union with someone, or something, outside ourselves, while retaining the separateness and integrity of our own selves. It is a sharing, a communion, which permits the full unfolding of our own inner life. It is the active and

---

[50]Rank, *Beyond Psychology*, pp. 150, 159, 164, 167, 190.
[51]Fromm, *The Sane Society*, pp. 27-66.

creative relatedness of ourselves to our fellowman, to nature and to ourselves.

The second need is transcendence. Another significant aspect of the human situation is our "creatureliness," hence our need to transcend the state of the passive creature. We are thrown into this world, and removed from it again, without our consent. We are endowed with the ability to create life, and this presupposes activity, care and love for that which we create. We are driven, then, by the urge to transcend the role of the creature with its "accidentalness" and passivity, and become a "creator."

Our third need is for rootedness. We are able to dispense with natural roots only insofar as we find *new human* roots. It is then and only then that we can feel at home again in this world. As adults, though fully grown and independent of parents, we still need warmth, help and protection. Reason, love, human solidarity and justice are values we must cultivate if we are to transform our world into a "truly human home."

We need, fourth, a sense of identity. Because we are endowed with reason and imagination we need to form a self-concept — we must be able to say with conviction, "I am I." The need for a sense of identity stems from the very condition of human existence, and is the source of our most intense strivings.

Finally, we need a frame of orientation. Our reason and imagination lead us to the necessity of orienting ourselves to our world intellectually. This need exists on two levels: a need to have some framework regardless of whether it is true or not; and a need to be in touch with reality by reason, thus being able to grasp the world objectively.

Love and freedom are the only answers to our deep needs. We, in modern society, have become free from all the primary bonds that traditionally have given meaning and security to life (i.e., the church, the State, even duty, patriotism and conscience). But we cannot bear our isolation; we feel helpless. The unity of our world has broken down; we have lost any point of orientation. Overcome by doubts and fears, we are driven to a new bondage, conformity.[52]

Fromm proffers an answer: we can be free and independent without being alone, and critical without being filled with doubts. Spontaneous activity emanating from an integrated personality, though relatively rare — except for artists, small children and a few others — is the way to positive freedom. Such spontaneous activity reunites us with our fellows, with nature, and with ourselves. Love, as the affirmation of and the union with others, is the indispensable element of this spontaneity.[53] All of our attempts to give and receive love are bound to fail unless we try most actively to develop our total personality. Satisfaction in individual love cannot be attained without the capacity to love our neighbor, nor without true humility, courage, faith and discipline. Love of neighbor and love of self go hand in hand. If it is a virtue to love our neighbor, it must be a virtue — and not a vice — to love ourselves. Love for and understanding of our own selves cannot be separated from respect, love and understanding for others.[54]

Fromm[55] insists:

> There is no more convincing proof that the injunction "Love thy neighbor as thyself" is the most important norm of living and that its violation is the basic cause of unhappiness and mental illness than the evidence gathered by the psychoanalyst. Whatever complaints the neurotic patient may have, whatever symptoms he may present are rooted in his inability to love, if we mean by love a capacity for the experience of concern, responsibility, respect and understanding of another person and the intense desire for that other person's growth. . . .

> Psychoanalysis also shows that love . . . cannot be restricted to one person. Anyone who loves only one person

---

[52]Fromm, *Escape from Freedom*, pp. 256-57.
[53]*Ibid.*, pp. 257-61.
[54]Erich Fromm, *The Art of Loving*, A Bantam Sixty. (New York: Bantam Books, 1956), pp. vii, 49.
[55]Fromm, *Psychoanalysis and Religion*, pp. 86-87.

and does not love "his neighbor" demonstrates that his love for one person is an attachment of submission or of domination but not love. . . . The human reality behind the concept of man's love for God in humanistic religion is man's ability to love productively, to love without greed, without submission and domination, to love from the fullness of his personality.

A Limited View of Existentialism

Existential psychotherapy is a modification of psychoanalysis begun by a number of Europeans dissatisfied with orthodox psychoanalysis. Contending that society's most perplexing problem is our "feeling of alienation" from the world coupled with a loss of the sense of identity or belonging, they maintain that psychoanalysis has often tended to increase the total problem by fragmenting human personality still further. Existentialism emphasizes that we *exist* first and foremost, and then we decide what we will be. Our own choices determine what we will become, since even a refusal to choose is a choice. We are led in therapy, then, back to the original or basic choice that has led to our maladjustive behavior. The purpose of existential psychoanalysis is to comprehend us, as persons seeking clarification, in our uniquenesses. Our goals and values are studied carefully. Once our "self" has found its own being, says Binswanger, and become oriented to its world, the goal is to achieve a being-beyond-itself, a sort of transcendence through love. This love, which closely resembles knowledge, reconciles our rational concepts and emotional feelings so as to produce in us a feeling of unity with our fellowman.[56]

For Sartre, existential psychoanalysis is a method designed to bring to light the subjective choices by which we make ourselves individuals.[57] While he has applied his philosophical postulates in the psychological areas of emotion and imagination, he has failed to arrive at a consistent psychology of

[56]Ruch, *Psychology and Life*, 6th ed., p. 242.
[57]Winn, *A Concise Dictionary of Existentialism*, p. 84.

personality. Viktor Frankl,[58] hoping to supply this omission, has conceived a system which completes and supplements both psychoanalysis and individual psychology.

Frankl's school of existential analysis, called logotherapy, identifies the striving to find meaning in our lives as our primary motivational force.[59] This "will-to-meaning" is regarded as a peculiarly human phenomenon, since animals do not concern themselves with meaning. We find meaning through self-realization which involves both the freedom to choose a course of action and responsibility to choose in such a way as to further our spiritual values. Logotherapy, then, lays particular stress upon the development of our spiritual and ethical values.

Frankl portrays us as rational creatures; he believes we are capable of self-control and direction, and is convinced that our proper perfection is to be found in the realm of the spirit. He makes the dignity of man the cornerstone of his structure of thought. Traditional psychotherapy avows to free us from psychological as well as physiological obstacles to proper functioning, and to help bring to our awareness unconscious processes. Logotherapy purports to free us not simply *from* something but *into* a freedom for self-actualization and self-determination. Existential therapy forces us to choose, for once we accept responsibility we will look for a way to fulfill our own aspirations. Although both Adler and Freud have viewed human activity as caused by biological, sociological and psychological factors, Frankl builds upon the premise that we must come to terms with such influences, for we have the freedom either to submit to them or to control them and mold them for our own use. If we are normal human beings we will sense a direction to our lives and a consistency of purpose which transcends the demands of the moment. If we forget this obligation and try to live only for

---

[58]Frankl, *The Doctor*, pp. 17-18.
[59]Edith Weisskopf-Joelson, "Some Comments on a Viennese School of Psychiatry," *Journal of Abnormal and Social Psychology* 51:701-03 (1955).

the present moment (as exemplified by the alcoholic) we pervert life.[60]

The fact that there is meaning in *parts* of the universe suggests some kind of "supermeaning," even though as finite creatures we cannot grasp a totality of meaning. Faith in this "supermeaning" is of great significance for psychological health; it is what makes us strong. It is obvious that pleasure is not the main motivator in life, for there is more displeasure than pleasure in every life. The meaning of life must reside in the realm of values and objectively real goals. It is through the realization of values we find meaning: creative values (achieving tasks), experiential values (experiencing something or someone in its or his uniqueness), and attitudinal values (facing suffering responsibly) (see pp. 114-15). To live is to suffer; to survive is to find meaning in that suffering. We have an obligation to actualize values as long as we live, and attitudinal values can always be achieved, even when creative and experiential values are not available to us. Our lives have a unique goal to which we must find our uniquely fitting pattern. The more we experience life as a task, the more we shall realize the meaning of life. From a religious perspective, life, more than being simply a task, is a mission that demands fulfillment.[61]

Our search for meaning is a primary force — not a "secondary rationalization" of instinctual drives. Its meaning is unique and specific in that it must and can be fulfilled by us alone; only then does it achieve a significance which will satisfy our will to meaning. While some authors contend that meanings and values are nothing but defense mechanisms, reaction formations, and sublimations, Frankl insists that he would not be willing to live for the sake of his defense mechanisms, nor be ready to die for the sake of his reaction formations. Some of us, however, are able to do both for the sake of our ideals and values. The meaning of our existence is not invented by us but rather discovered. We do not behave

---

[60]Arnold and Gasson, *The Human Person*, pp. 464-65, 477-78, 481.
[61]*Ibid.*, pp. 465-68.

morally to have a good conscience; we do so for the sake of a cause to which we commit ourselves or for someone we love, or for the sake of our God.[62]

There is nothing in the world that would so effectively help us survive even the worst conditions as the knowledge that there is a meaning to our lives. In the Nazi concentration camps those who knew that there was a task waiting for them to fulfill were most apt to survive. We should not be hesitant, therefore, about challenging our fellows with a potential meaning for them to fulfill. Equilibrium or homeostasis is not only a pitifully low level of motivation to strive for but is a dangerous misconception. What we need is the striving and struggling for some goal worthy of us. The task of the logotherapist is to broaden our visual field so that we comprehend the whole spectrum of meaning and values.[63]

Every age has its own collective neurosis and therefore needs its own psychotherapy to cope with it. The existential vacuum that is the mass neurosis of our time is best described as a form of nihilism; for nihilism may be defined as the belief that being is without meaning.[64] The root of distressing disorders is the failure to find meaning in and a sense of responsibility for our existence.

THE VIEW OF THE BEHAVIORIST

Although meaningfulness and purposefulness in living are taken for granted by most people, behaviorists deny them. Z. Y. Kuo, a distinguished Chinese behaviorist, argues that the concept of purpose is a lazy substitute for careful and detailed analysis. With an increased understanding of elementary stimuli patterns and the physiological facts, as well as with a clearer insight into the behavior-history, the concept of purpose (in whatever form) will eventually disappear. As human machines we behave in certain ways because environmental stimulation has forced us to do so.[65]

---

[62]Frankl, *Man's Search for Meaning*, pp. 99-102.
[63]*Ibid.*, pp.105-07, 112.
[64]*Ibid.*, p. 131.
[65]Weatherhead, *Psychology, Religion and Healing*, p. 288.

The term "behaviorism," as introduced by J. B. Watson, is the view that conduct may be precisely determined if we know and successfully manipulate all of the psychological factors impinging upon the individual. It is possible, he insists, to define psychology as the science of behavior and never go back upon that definition, refusing to use terms like consciousness, mental states, mind, will and imagery. Psychology progresses only insofar as it is able to free itself from the "trammels of consciousness and introspection." Freedom, imagination, mind, feeling and will have to be ignored. Stimulus and response, and the drives of instinct and habit are the really important concepts. Psychology is to be an exact science, and as such is able to control behavior and predict conduct. No introspection is allowed. Psychology thus can be as objective a science as any other.[66]

By observing overt behavior in carefully controlled experiments we are able to obtain all data necessary for understanding human personality. Psychology, specifically, is to be the science of behavior, not of consciousness. Psychologists have introduced unnecessary mystery, Watson observes, by replacing the mind or soul by the inaccessible brain. Behaviorism, rather than making a fetish of the brain, must keep its eyes fixed on the sense organs, muscles and glands. No matter how complex it is, behavior can be analyzed and described in terms of stimulus-response bonds. In a famous and often criticized statement Watson declares that if given a dozen healthy, well-formed infants, and his own special world to raise them in, he would guarantee to take any one at random and train him to become any kind of specialist — rich man, poor man, beggar-man, thief; doctor, lawyer, merchant, chief — regardless of his talents, tendencies, abilities or race.[67]

The newborn starts off as a bundle of basic reflexes, which are gradually built, through maturation and reactive behavior within the environment, into more complex patterns,

[66]*Ibid.*, pp. 294-95.
[67]Hildreth Cross, *An Introduction to Psychology* (Grand Rapids: Zondervan Publishing House, 1952), pp. 98-101.

skills and motor activities. Thorndike's outstanding contribution is the "law of effect," which maintains that learning is hastened when associated with a total situation that is predominantly pleasant, but retarded if the associated aspects of that situation are unpleasant.[68]

Pavlov's discovery of the conditioned reflex is seen by Watson and Thorndike as highly supportive of their theories. He has demonstrated[69] that if he feeds hungry dogs tasty foods, over a period of time, preceded by the sounding of a gong (or the shining of a red lamp or the starting of a metronome ticking) the sensory stimuli will cause the salivary glands of the dogs to secrete even when no food is around. The dogs secrete saliva when a gong is sounded on a certain note, say C major, but not if the gong sounds on a note a semitone higher or lower on the musical scale. They salivate exactly thirty minutes after the presentation of the stimulus, while no reaction is obtained even at the twenty-ninth minute. Pavlov's succinct conclusion from these experiments which have fascinated psychologists around the world: behavior lies wholly in physiology.

THE VIEW OF THE HUMANIST

Building upon such concepts as self-consistency, self-reference, success motivation and the avoidance of failure, A. H. Maslow, along with other such notables as Carl Rogers and Sidney Jourard, has become concerned with the development of our potentials to the full. For such a pervasive type of motive the term "self-actualization" has been adopted, originally by Carl Jung. By self-actualization Maslow means the development of our full individuality, with all of the parts somehow in harmony. This term (and related ones such as creative becoming, etc.) is being used by psychologists who criticize most contemporary motivational theory as being too narrow and "episodic" rather than being concerned with the more profound and pervasive aspects of our

---

[68]*Ibid.*, pp. 101-02.
[69]Weatherhead, *Psychology, Religion and Healing*, pp. 295-96.

aspirations.[70] This pressure toward self-actualization Maslow variously describes as the "will to health," the urge to grow and the quest for identity.[71]

In the *modern* approach, as developed by Goldstein, Fromm, Horney, Rogers, Lecky and Allport, as well as Maslow, we concern ourselves not only with what we *are*, but what we *may become*. We focus not only upon surface actualities, but potentialities as well. Ideas such as homeostasis, equilibrium, adaptation, self-preservation, defense and adjustment are supplanted by more positive concepts. Motivational theory must deal with the highest capacities of our healthiest and strongest citizens as well as with the "defensive maneuvers of crippled spirits." Instead of using the motivational life of neurotic sufferers as a paradigm for healthy motivation, we must comprehend the all-encompassing goals and supreme concerns of the greatest and finest people in history.[72]

Maslow[73] has developed a hierarchy of emotional needs which takes as its starting point the physiological drives (hunger, thirst, etc.). It is useless to argue for any specific list of fundamental physiological needs, he says, for we could identify nearly any specific number we might wish. Regardless of which list is adopted, the physiological needs must be satisfied first. Second are safety needs, which refer to our demands for an environment that is safe, orderly and manageable. Such disturbances as loss of bodily support, loud noises and other sudden unexpected stimuli that upset our equilibrium as infants are phenomena that prevent this need from being met. Next are belongingness and love needs, which refer specifically to our affectional relationships with our family, friends and society, and, generally, to our need

---

[70]Hilgard and Atkinson, *Introduction to Psychology*, p. 159.

[71]Abraham H. Maslow, "Some Basic Propositions of a Growth and Self-Actualization Psychology," in *Perceiving, Behaving, Becoming: A New Focus for Education*, 1962 Yearbook, Association for Supervision and Curriculum Development (Washington: Association for Supervision and Curriculum Development, 1962), p. 35.

[72]Maslow, *Motivation and Personality*, pp. 79, 342, 367.

[73]*Ibid.*, pp. 80-91.

for a place in the group. Further up the scale are the esteem needs which refer to the desire for a stable, firmly-based, typically high evaluation of ourselves, for self-respect or self-esteem and for the esteem of others. Esteem needs may be divided into two categories: desire for reputation, status, dominance, and recognition on the one hand, and strength, mastery and competence on the other.

The higher level needs are self-actualization needs, (see below) cognitive needs and aesthetic needs. Cognitive needs are needs for broad understanding and for an integrated set of values. Aesthetic needs are the least known and explored of all those discussed. For some, at least, there is a basic aesthetic need, as reflected by the fact that we become "sick" from ugliness, and are "cured" again by beautiful surroundings.[74]

The essence of Maslow's theory of motivation is that when one need is reasonably well satisfied the next prepotent (higher) need emerges in turn to dominate the conscious life and to serve as the center of behavior organization since gratified needs are not active motivators. Under conditions of unsatisfied lower needs we may "lose" the higher needs.[75]

Maslow does not wish to create the impression that after one set of needs is entirely met another emerges. Normally, we are partially satisfied and unsatisfied in all our basic needs at the same time. There are, as it were, decreasing percentages of satisfaction as we go up the hierarchy of prepotency. For example, we may experience 85 per cent satisfaction in our physiological needs, 70 per cent in safety needs, 50 per cent in love needs, 40 per cent in self-esteem needs, and 10 per cent in self-actualization needs. But even when all our lower needs are satisfied we often experience a basic restlessness unless we are doing that for which we are fitted. Musicians must make music; artists must paint. What we *can* be we *must* be. The need for self-actualization, or self-fulfillment is the tendency to become actualized in what we are

---

[74]Maslow, *Motivation and Personality*, p. 97.
[75]Ansbacher and Ansbacher, *Individual Psychology*, p. 124.

potentially. It is the desire to become more than what we are; we are to become everything we are capable of becoming.[76]

In a more recent classification,[77] Maslow divides motives into two classes: the deficiency or lower motives, specified as D motives, and the being or higher motives, called B motives. In general, motives lower in the hierarchy are aroused through deficiencies and are indeed urgent determiners of behavior when their satisfaction is lacking. The higher motives (B motives) come into play chiefly when the D motives have been cared for adequately. To function at our highest level our survival needs and our normal social requirements must be met but, beyond that, we may expect to reach forward to great heights of personality attainment.

To give empirical support to his concepts, Maslow has attempted to locate self-actualizing persons.[78] His selection has not followed the ordinary sampling methods. While over 3000 potential cases have been reviewed, only a few have been chosen as representative of self-actualization. Students selected represent the healthiest one per cent of the college population.

The overall criteria for being chosen were the apparent lack of neurotic or psychotic trends and the obvious full use of talents, capacities, and potentialities. Among the eminent personalities selected were Lincoln, Jefferson, Einstein, Eleanor Roosevelt, Jane Addams, Williams James and Spinoza. After careful biographical study of the lives of these famous personalities and the case studies of a few contemporaries, Maslow arrived at a composite of self-actualizing people. A listing of the fifteen specific traits making up this composite is included on page 124.

Self-actualized (or more accurately, self-actualizing) people generally feel safe and unanxious, accepted, loved and loving, respect-worthy and respected, and are persons who have worked out their philosophical, religious or axiological prob-

---

[76]Maslow, *Motivation and Personality*, pp. 91, 100-01.
[77]Hilgard and Atkinson, *Introduction to Psychology*, p. 159.
[78]Maslow, *Motivation and Personality*, pp. 199-224.

lems. They have developed or are developing to the full stature of their capabilities. Their physiological needs, as well as their safety, belongingness and love needs, are well met. Their needs for self-actualization, cognition and aesthetic satisfaction are in the process of being met. They have a heightened appreciation for life, others and themselves, a detachment from the conforming aspects of culture, and an originality or creativity that ranks them far above the level of their fellows.

They possess a quality that may be called "humility" of a certain type. While they are well aware of their own worth, .there is no humbleness of the cringing or designing type. They are aware of the little they know in comparison with what could be known or what others know. Thus, it is possible for them without pose to be honestly respectful and even humble before those who can teach them something they do not know or have a skill they do not possess.[79]

Self-actualized individuals are not defensive, but loving, spontaneous and open. In their love relationships they affirm the individuality of others, are eager for their growth, have an essential respect for their individuality and uniqueness of personality and rejoice in their accomplishments as much as their own.

They fall in love much as we react to our first appreciative perception of great music; we love it and are awed and overwhelmed by it. The consequent reactions are to enjoy, admire, delight in, contemplate and appreciate rather than *use*. They love because they are loving persons, in the same way that they are kind, honest, natural, i.e., because it is their nature to be so spontaneously.[80]

Peak experiences, defined as incidents bringing a strong sense of happiness and fulfillment, are part of Maslow's concept of self-actualization.[81] These are experiences of temporary nonstriving, are non self-centered, and are referred to as times of perfection, ecstasy and goal-attainment. By asking

[79]Arnold and Gasson, *The Human Person*, p. 187.
[80]Maslow, *Motivation and Personality*, pp. 239, 244, 249, 252-56.
[81]Hilgard and Atkinson, *Introduction to Psychology*, p. 160.

some 190 college students to describe their peak experiences
he has developed a list of "B-values" (being motives) which
includes wholeness, perfection and self-sufficiency, along
with such standard values as beauty, goodness and truth. As
a result of studying descriptions of peak experiences Maslow
has more recently modified his position. He maintains that
nearly everyone, at some time or other, has a peak experience, during which he is self-actualized. The "consistent self-
actualizers," whom Maslow has identified in his earlier writings, would appear to differ only in that their peak experiences
occur more frequently, intensely and perfectly than others'.
Peak experiences are of significance in that they enrich life's
meaning and are treasured in memory by their recipients.

A Christian Perspective

The major strivings of our generation may be summarized
in three words: pleasure, materialism and popularity. For
many of us, the dominant motivation in life is the pursuit of
pleasure — the obtaining of sensual satisfaction from a gratification of the instincts and drives. Others among us orient
our strivings toward the acquisition of things — to satisfy a
need for success, status or a superiority over others. A third
group strives for popularity, acceptance and security which
we attain by conformity. These are precisely the strivings
declared as the dominant motivators by Freud, Adler and
Fromm, respectively.

Some might attempt to reconcile these three by declaring
that happiness is the goal of all of us — and that it may take
any one or all of these forms — or a dozen others we have not
mentioned. The goal of happiness, however, falls far short
of being a worthy motivator, if ours is truly a Christian perspective. Happiness is the by-product of self-respect and
legitimate, unselfish accomplishment, not a deliberate goal toward which we consciously strive.

What is our stance as Christians in the midst of a culture
characterized by an obsessive seeking for pleasure, happiness,
success, superiority, and the like? Is there the "beat of a dis-
tant drum" which calls us to a motivation different from

these? Is there a will to meaning (Frankl) or a will to immortality (Rank) that distinguishes our strivings as Christians from those of others? Is there a distinctiveness in the realm of axiology which Christianity provides? We answer these questions with a resounding "Yes" — a dynamic relationship with Jesus Christ projects ultimate meaning into life.

It is a moot question as to what proportion of our society is burdened down with what Frankl has called "noögenic neurosis."[82] We would contend that, in one sense, it is the affliction of every individual who has not made the choice in favor of Jesus Christ. Unless He brings meaning to our lives we wander through life aimlessly — and this is precisely what "noögenic neurosis" is. Christianity provides the antidote to this disease, the plus factor that makes living truly worthwhile. Sin — which always separates — prevents us from being reconciled to God. Similarly, it keeps us from being at one with ourselves and others. It produces a sense of isolation and estrangement. When God confronts us with our sins and we respond by seeking His pardon, a reconciliation is effected between ourselves and Him which provides the basis for a sense of acceptance or at-one-ment in our relationships with our fellows and within ourselves.

An initial encounter with Christ, then, provides a sense of direction for our motivation. Our day-to-day actions fortify and continually revitalize that goal. We are thus led along a glorious path that represents a fulfilling of His plan for our lives.

As we grow in His likeness we acquire a vision of our spiritual mission which unfolds in unanticipated and diverse directions. Through prayer, the reading of Scripture, instruction (through preaching, counseling, etc.) and a host of other ways coordinated by the Holy Spirit, a vision begins to unfold of our unique place and contribution within the Kingdom of God. We slowly realize that a full dedication of our lives is demanded to fulfill that mission. This dedication is reasonable, for unless we give ourselves to Him fully

---

[82]Frankl, *Man's Search for Meaning*, p. 102.

we cannot appropriate the abundant life He wishes to bring, nor can we receive the empowering to make us effective in our living. Such a vision is highly personal, conveying to us how we can be relevant and effective in our sphere of influence, whether narrow or broad. Of course there are obstacles mitigating against our success, circumstances seemingly impossible to overcome. St. Peter, walking on the water toward Christ, was actually succeeding at the impossible until he looked at the waves and *away from Christ*.

The Divine image must remain central in our vision. We need the kind of vision that Isaiah had in the temple — of a great and all-powerful God, high and lifted up (Isaiah 6:1-4). The scales must be removed frequently from our eyes, as they were from Elisha's servant's eyes, so that we can be assured that the forces of God are mightier than the forces of the enemy that rim the canyon of our particular battle arena (II Kings 6:17). When our vision is clarified it becomes obvious that He who is in us is greater than he who is in the world (I John 4:4).

To relate ourselves to God effectively is to avail ourselves of the resources of the universe. Greater things than even Jesus' own earthly works we shall do, He assures us, because He was to return to His Father (John 14:12). We can do all things through Christ who strengthens us (Philippians 4:13). If we ask it shall be given us; if we seek we shall find (Matthew 7:7); if we trust He shall supply our every need according to His riches in glory (Philippians 4:19). All things are ours and we are Christ's and Christ is God's (I Corinthians 3:22-23).

We must go a step beyond receiving a vision of His resources and adequacy; we must translate such a vision into action. We are to say with Isaiah, "I have seen the Lord" — and follow it with, "Here am I; send me" (Isaiah 6:5-8). The action side of Christianity is as important as the vision side. We are to be doers of the Word, not hearers only, James 1:22 declares. To continue to receive from God and fail to share of the abundance received leads to spiritual leanness and defeat.

A scientist does not create cosmic energy, but liberates, concentrates and uses it, Fosdick reminds us. To change the figure, we are to release God's power from "unfailing reservoirs." Such power does not originate in us, it *flows through* us; plenty of water is available. When the channels are open our strength shall not fail, for output is balanced by intake. Great living springs, like a fountain, from within.[83] Transformed and renewed in mind, it is not we who release power; in the truest sense it is Christ, living in us, who releases His power through us.

Patterning our ways after Christ's may sound somewhat static, unimaginative and uncreative. Life in Christ, however, does not mean becoming carbon copies of model saints on the order of the Apostle Paul or St. Francis of Assisi. We have been created individually and are different from everyone else who ever lived. We are to assume our *own* individuality, creatively, guided by the Holy Spirit, in terms of *our* interests, aptitudes, experiences, culture, environment and intimate associations. The knowledge that God creates every snowflake differently should serve to reassure us that He desires us to be our uniquely developing and maturing, individual selves. As a loving heavenly Father, God is delighted when we as His children achieve at or near the peak of our potentialities and become more and more what we are capable of becoming. Such a viewpoint becomes increasingly plausible as we develop a more profound concept of the nature of God Himself.

God has revealed Himself as a master architect, designer, landscaper, builder, artist and sculpturer. As we understand something of the breadth of His insight, His versatility, His capabilities, His achievements in the universe, His brilliant planning and His execution of these plans, we begin to take on, in a measure, some of these qualities. Our creativeness unfolds as we enter into partnership with the Creator. This is not dissimilar to our tendency as children to pattern our lives after admired persons of our family and broader acquaintance and, a bit later, those of historical and public prom-

---

[83]Harry Emerson Fosdick, *On Being A Real Person*, A Harper Chapelbook. (New York: Harper and Row, 1943), pp. 213-14.

inence, identifying with the most admirable personalities available. As Christians we discover *our* identity by patterning our lives after God, or, more specifically, after His Son, Jesus Christ, Who is made known to us through the Scriptures as well as through the personal revelation of the Holy Spirit. We echo the words of St. Paul: "For to me to live is Christ" (Philippians 1:21). In such a spirit we begin cultivating the attributes of humility, self-discipline, purity of thought, singleness of motive, and the like. Concurrently, we concentrate on developing our social interrelationships toward their fullest capacities. To love our neighbor as we do ourselves involves a cultivation of such social and Christian graces as kindness, thoughtfulness, helpfulness, forgiveness, mercifulness, unselfishness and patience.

Such a concept of life in Christ hardly seems stultifying, unimaginative and uncreative. Granted that we are human, earthen and weak vessels, we declare that we are vessels for a noble use, repositories for the presence of the Almighty Himself. Collectively, as the body of Christ, we are to build His church in the world. Some of us will be apostles (leaders), some prophets, some teachers, and others, just "helpers." We are to seek His gifts in order to build effectively: prophecy and wisdom, leadership and administration, healing and edifying, faith and the working of miracles, etc. (I Corinthians 12:9-10; 28-31). In our seeking and developing these gifts, we are directed to the greatest gift of all — love, as it is epitomized in Christ Himself.

To change the figure from the vessel, we are to run successfully the race that is set before us, looking unto Christ as the "pacemaker," "forerunner" and "finisher" in the race of life (Hebrews 12:1-2). Our Coach directs our running, provides our impetus, lights and maps out our pathway so that we will finish our course despite all of the obstacles arrayed against us. We press toward "the prize of the upward call of God" (Philippians 3:14) — as the faraway goal — and strive toward the successful attainment of the "here and now" goals of developing perfection of life and motive and of increasingly loving and compassionate interrelationships.

St. Paul's admonition to the Philippians serves as the cap-
stone to our motivation: "Remember always to live as Christians should, so that . . . you are standing side by side with
one strong purpose — to tell the Good News. . ." (Philippians
1:27, *Living Letters*). We are to point others to Him — His
person, His work and His relevance; His ability to do great
things for and in them. Our personalities are to be outgoing
and redemptive; we are to alleviate need and suffering wher-
ever we find them; we are to point the way to the One
who is The Way of life, hope, and love.

To embark on such an adventure is to experience, at times,
failure and frustration — even conflict. Perfection seems remote and unattainable. But our eyes remain riveted on the
goal; our spirit stays attuned to the One who can lead us
unerringly to that goal — and we continue to narrow the
gap between the ideal and the real by increasingly becoming
what we ought to be as well as becoming progressively
more aware of what we yet can become.

To be motivated toward such "becoming" has many implications for mental health. In the final chapter, we will
examine the major contributions toward a philosophy of mental health and conclude with a "model" of Christian growth
that will provide a concrete goal toward which we can strive
meaningfully and joyfully.

Discussion Questions

1. How much of Freud's pleasure principle is applicable to a Christian philosophy? (Is Christianity followed because it is more pleasurable than its alternatives?)

2. Should Christianity contribute to our being more introvertive or less?

3. How can we maintain our freedom in the face of pressures toward conformity by society, friends, the church, etc.?

4. React to the statement: "The strivings of our generation may be summarized in three words — pleasure, materialism and popularity" (Page 90).

5. How are the strivings of the Christian different from those cited in the above question?

6. Are the peak experiences of Christians different from others' peak experiences?

IV

The Dynamics of Wholeness

INTRODUCTION

The three previous chapters point toward a concept of mental health. Our viewpoint from the beginning has been that we as human beings possess elements of both good and evil. Therefore, we must learn how to come to grips with the "guilt" side of our nature but at the same time how to affirm and build our inherent "motivation" dimension toward fulfillment in life. As the old song so aptly puts it, "Ya gotta accentuate the positive; eliminate the negative." The positive side we have been calling motivation; the negative, guilt.

A host of psychologists have dealt with the subject of this chapter. The task before us is to sift through the most significant of their ideas and build upon them a Christian philosophy of mental health.

The chapter follows, again, the basic pattern of highlighting the major alternatives or viewpoints about mental health, beginning with the psychoanalytic writers, continuing with Fromm and Allport, proceeding with the existentialists and the humanists, and concluding with a Christian perspective.

THE MAJOR PSYCHOANALYTIC WRITERS

Sigmund Freud

Freud deals very little with the superstructure of personality. His concern, by his own admission, has been with the

97

basement and substructures of our being. Nevertheless, a brief section is included on Sigmund Freud because frequent reference is made in the literature to his concepts, both by those who find some support for their own ideas and those who use him as the point of take-off for erecting their own theoretical superstructures. Freud focuses almost exclusively upon intrapsychic life, whereas many later theorists deal extensively with our interrelationships with society. Christian writers, along with some others, add a third dimension, our relationship to God.

Freud acknowledges[1] the importance of strengthening the ego, making it increasingly independent of the superego, widening its field of vision, and extending its organization so that it may take over new portions of the id. "Where id was, there shall ego be," is his succinct statement.

To be mentally healthy, according to Freud, we are to develop an awareness of unconscious motivations and a self-control based on insight.[2] We must recognize the basic, unalterable contradiction between human nature and society. Within us are two driving compulsions: pleasure, broadly conceived, and aggression. The aim we all follow, he would have us believe, is to have complete sexual freedom. Having found that sexual love gives us life's greatest possible gratification, and thus has become virtually a prototype of all happiness, we are impelled to seek happiness along the path of sexual relations, thus making genital eroticism the central focus of our lives.[3] The problem of sex is a complex one of adjusting tensions within our personality — the tensions of the sexual urge, of the social requirements as they appear to us, and the influence of our moral training.[4]

Mental health is the full achievement of the capacity for

---

[1]Freud, *New Introductory Lectures*, p. 112.

[2]Morris S. Schwartz and Charlotte Green Schwartz, "Mental Health: The Concept," *International Encyclopedia of the Social Sciences*, X, 216.

[3]Sigmund Freud, *Civilization and its Discontents*, trans. by Joan Riviere. (London: The Hogarth Press, Limited, 1951), p. 69.

[4]May, *The Art of Counseling*, pp. 31-32.

love, attained when and if the libido development reaches the genital stage. Maturity is the bodily manner in which we achieve our principal satisfactions. Those of us who, since childhood, have shown dominant characteristics of any one of the three early stages of psychosexual development (oral, anal or phallic) are "fixated" at that level. Those of us who give evidence of a higher level of functioning may encounter a life crisis and be unable to maintain our progress. If we seek security in earlier and more deeply ingrained patterns of emotional behavior, we are labelled "regressed" or "retrogressed."[5]

Freudian psychoanalysis never really regards adults as "adult."[6] Nor can Freud accept a truly religious sentiment within. We need no illusory God, he says, because such a need is an attempt to regain intensity and intimacy in the parent-child relationship. We are strong enough within ourselves to combat the "crushing supremacy" of life and to ease the suffering of being alive.[7] Our religious experiences are interpreted as regressions into a stage of "limitless narcissism."[8] The analytic process, then, is designed to liberate us from such regressions so that we are able to make better choices for ourselves.

Alfred Adler

Adler is the first of a long procession of those who disagree vehemently with Freud's concepts of mental health.[9] He attempts to develop a humanistic approach to personality that restores to the human race, as it were, the sense of dignity and worth that Freudian psychoanalysis had largely destroyed.

[5]Norman Tallent, *Psychological Perspectives on the Person,* Insight Series. (Princeton: D. VanNostrand Company, 1967), p. 130.
[6]Gordon Allport, *Personality: A Psychological Interpretation* (New York: Henry Holt and Company, 1937), p. 216.
[7]Freeman and Small, *The Story of Psychoanalysis,* p. 123.
[8]Freud, *Civilization and Its Discontents,* p. 21.
[9]Hall and Lindzey, *Theories of Personality,* p. 125.

Adler insists that the goal of individual psychology is social adjustment. We become individuals only in a social context.[10] No mature person grows without cultivating a deep sense of fellowship with humanity and practicing the art of being human. We are social beings and demand to be dealt with as such. Taking his cue from the neurotic who is characterized by his inability to make connections with the world of people, he asserts that we cannot separate ourselves from our social group and remain healthy, for the very structure of personality is dependent upon "community." At any given instant, every one of us is dependent upon countless other people. Adler calls this interdependence the "love and logic that binds us all together."[11] The community is the best guarantee we have that the human race will continue to exist.[12]

The dynamic force within all of us is the striving for power, or the will to prestige; this is what gives us the impetus to break out of the web of social dependence and set ourselves, in ambition and vanity, above our fellowman. Inferiority feelings, originating in our childhood, force each of us into compensatory behavior in an effort to overcome our inferiority. This inferiority feeling, coupled with the will to prestige, supplies us with our prime source of motive power. The problem is to use this power, not in anti-social striving, which only destroys the social constellation, but in a way which constructively contributes to the well-being of our fellow humans.[13]

The striving for superiority, i.e., from minus to plus, never ceases.[14] In fact, it is the essence of our psyche. Each drive receives its power from the striving for completion.[15]

The key to the entire social process is to be found in the fact that we are always striving to find a situation in which

---

[10]Adler, *The Science of Living*, p. 199.
[11]May, *The Art of Counseling*, pp. 62-63.
[12]Alfred Adler, *Understanding Human Nature*, trans. by Walter Béran Wolfe. (New York: Greenburg, 1927), p. 29.
[13]May, *The Art of Counseling*, pp. 63-65.
[14]Adler, *The Science of Living*, pp. 79-80.
[15]Hall and Lindzey, *Theories of Personality*, p. 120.

we excel. As long as we temper this striving with social interest, we are on the useful side of life, and we accomplish good.[16] It is normal to want to be superior, to want to succeed, and as long as this striving is expressed in work it does not lead along a path to neurosis.[17]

In Adler's early writings,[18] we humans are pictured as driven by an insatiable lust for power and domination in order to overcome our hidden yet deep-seated feeling of inferiority. In his mature thought, however, he describes us as being motivated by social interest, which causes us to subordinate private ambition to the public welfare.

Courage is essential to healthy living. Through it we are relieved of the compulsion of our inferiority feeling and do not need to strive against our fellows, but are willing to cooperate unselfishly with the group. Along with courage, the highest virtues are social interest and cooperation. These attributes mark the healthy ones among us who realize and cheerfully accept our social responsibility. By expressing ourselves in socially constructive ways we are able to realize ourselves and become socially "integrated." Adler makes social adjustment the criterion of personality adequacy.[19]

Adler's assumption that personality grows as simply and naturally as plants toward perfection requiring only the removal of obstructions, is a view reminiscent of Rousseau's concept of the nature of man.[20] Such a position (described in Chapter 1) is not taken seriously by most psychologists today outside the humanistic tradition.

Personality uniqueness is a recurring theme in Adler's later writings. Each of us has a "style of life," but no two of us develop the same style. While we all pursue the same goal (superiority), there are innumerable ways of attaining it. Some of us develop our intellect, while others strive for athletic prowess, and still others aspire to musical accomplish-

[16]Adler, *The Science of Living*, p. 74.
[17]*Ibid.*, pp. 96-97.
[18]Hall and Lindzey, *Theories of Personality*, p. 124.
[19]May, *The Art of Counseling*, pp. 36, 66.
[20]*Ibid.*, p. 69.

ment, etc. Regardless of the unique plan, all of our behavior springs from our style of life. This style of life is formed by age four or five, and from then on our experiences are assimilated and employed according to this specific style.[21]

Our creative self determines our individual style of life, i.e., we construct our personality out of the raw materials of heredity and experience. Heredity gives us certain abilities, while environment provides the impressions. Heredity and environment, along with the manner in which we experience them, are the building blocks we use in developing a philosophy of life. It is this philosophy of life which determines our relationship to our environment. This creative self endows life with true meaning and helps transform the facts of our existence into a personality that is dynamic, personal and unique.[22]

Carl Jung

Self-realization, or self-actualization, is the ultimate goal in analytical psychology. In self-actualization, the personality moves toward a perfect equilibrium of forces in which there is a harmonious blending of all aspects of personality.[23] Self-realization is seen by Jung as the major way of providing meaning in life, as well as of forming character.[24]

We constantly progress (or at least attempt to progress) from a less complete stage of development to a more complete stage. This growth is an unfolding of our inherited "undifferentiated wholeness."[25] Wholeness of personality is attained when opposites are reconciled and the conscious and unconscious are joined together. Our unconscious can never be made completely conscious, so that wholeness is always relative and thus constitutes a life-long challenge.[26]

---

[21]Adler, *The Science of Living*, pp. 61-63, 102, 118.
[22]Hall and Lindzey, *Theories of Personality*, pp. 124-25.
[23]*Ibid.*, p. 96.
[24]Jolan Jacobi, *The Psychology of Jung*, trans. by K. W. Bash. (New Haven: Yale University Press, 1943), p. 125.
[25]Hall and Lindzey, *Theories of Personality*, pp. 95-99.
[26]Jacobi, *The Psychology of Jung*, pp. 99-100.

Sometime during our adult development, roughly between the ages of thirty-five and forty-five, a "radical transvaluation" occurs, which is the most decisive event in our entire lifetime. In this transition, biological interests fade and a new set of interests emerges. We become more introverted and wise; we have less physical and mental vigor and impulsiveness. Our values shift to the social, religious, civic and philosophical realms. We are, in short, transformed into spiritual persons.[27]

This transition, or "individuation of the self," frequently comes about after we feel life to be meaningless.[28] It is a "realization of the self," or "finding the God within."[29] To have a healthy, integrated personality, we must become a "four square person," i.e., we must develop equally and to the maximum the four forms of psychic activity: thinking, feeling, sensation and intuition.[30] Individuation, Jung contends, is becoming our own innermost, final, incomparable uniqueness; our own self.[31]

The individuation process is a psychological journey; it can be an agonizing and treacherous path; in fact, it may at times seem to wind around in circles. Experience indicates that the truest description would be that of a spiral. If we are fortunate, we will attain, in the end, the self.[32]

Jung's writing contains many allusions to the highest experiences we can attain in our quest toward wholeness. He identifies as the four highest human achievements faith, hope, love and insight, which, while they come through experience, are "gifts of grace."[33]

There is a transcendent function within us that unites the opposite trends of the various systems within and impels us toward the goal of perfect wholeness. This transcendent

[27]Hall and Lindzey, *Theories of Personality*, pp. 97-98.
[28]Fordham, *An Introduction to Jung's Psychology*, p. 78.
[29]Freeman and Small, *The Story of Psychoanalysis*, p. 134.
[30]Arnold and Gasson, *The Human Person*, p. 510.
[31]Jacobi, *The Psychology of Jung*, pp. 100-01.
[32]Fordham, *An Introduction to Jung's Psychology*, p. 79.
[33]Jung, *Modern Man in Search of a Soul*, p. 261.

function "wins out," in the second half of life, over the drive
for sexuality and self-assertion.[34]

Religious faith, Jung repeatedly asserts, is essential to mental wholeness. This viewpoint, however, represents a shifting
over a lifetime in this great psychiatrist's insights.[35] Moving
from a position of "accepting" religion's role in society, he
later begins to recognize it as having genuine psychological
value as well, and finally he declares that the religious function may be the agent through which we may reach our
highest moments in life and our highest levels of development.

Perhaps the most frequently quoted statement by any psychologist about the significance of religion is this one by
Jung:[36]

> Among all my patients in the second half of life . . . there
> has not been one whose problem in the last resort was
> not that of finding a religious outlook on life. It is safe to
> say that every one of them fell ill because he had lost
> that which the living religions of every age have given to
> their followers, and none of them has been really healed
> who did not regain his religious outlook.

We must realize that the God Jung writes about is simply
the God-image within us. To sense the God-image or archetype is the most vital and overwhelming experience that can
happen to us. His study of the archetypes of the collective
unconscious has led him to conclude that we possess a natural
religious function and that our psychic health and stability
depend on a proper balance between this function and the
expression of our instincts.[37]

The God within, residing in the deepest levels of the collective unconscious, is the only God there is for Jung. His
explanation of religious experience is woefully incomplete.

---

[34]Fordham, *An Introduction to Jung's Psychology*, p. 88.
[35]Raymond Hostie, *Religion and the Psychology of Jung*, trans. by
G. R. Lamb. (New York: Sheed and Ward, 1957), pp. 144-47.
[36]Jung, *Modern Man in Search of a Soul*, p. 264.
[37]Fordham, *An Introduction to Jung's Psychology*, pp. 69, 73-74.

While we as Christians acknowledge that God is present in the deepest levels of our individual selves, He transcends human personality.[38] He is Person Himself, the Creator and Sustainer of the universe.

Otto Rank

Each of the "Big Four" in psychoanalysis, Freud, Adler, Jung and Rank, has reflected upon the spiritual core of our being. Each experiences it differently and gives it a different name. Rank labels it "the will to immortality." His ideas are much more positive than Freud's, and are a step beyond the social and cultural viewpoints of Adler and Jung.[39]

Rankian psychology stresses both our individuality and our social interdependence. Self-development is the aim of life; patients should make themselves into what they are, without force, justification, or the need to shift the responsibility for doing so.[40] Self-realization, on the other hand, comes through a social interdependence which, while influenced by the social milieu, exerts an influence upon that milieu and even transforms it.[41]

Rank's self-determination, or will, has a distinct bearing on mature adult personality. His views on active self-expression and our ability to control our adjustment and environment are in utter contrast to Freud's ego, which is virtually a play-ball of the forces of the id and superego. Will strengthens the personality in the direction of self-reliance, self-responsibility and self-realization through creativity.[42]

Rank's earlier writings[43] assert will to be a positive guiding force that organizes and integrates the self by creatively utilizing as well as inhibiting and controlling the instinctual drives. Willing is a resistance to compulsions; outer (parental

---

[38]May, *The Art of Counseling*, p. 218.
[39]Karpf, *The Psychology and Psychotherapy of Otto Rank*, p. 61.
[40]Rank, *Will Therapy*, p. 229.
[41]Karpf, *Psychology and Psychotherapy*, p. 60.
[42]*Ibid.*, p. 114.
[43]Arnold and Gasson, *The Human Person*, pp. 159-60.

demands) and inner (demands of the instincts). There are three levels of willing: the generalized defense of our self against its destruction; the striving for a particular goal out of envy and/or competition with others; and the establishment of and working toward our own standards and ideals.

Our will develops through three stages[44] in its striving for freedom. First, we accept as our own what previously external factors or internal drives have dictated 'that we accept. (Most of us remain, Rank insists, on this level all of our lives.) There is no great opportunity for creativity here, but neither is there much occasion for conflict.

Second, we will as our own what is usually contrary to early coercions. We exert a "counter will," willing that which is contrary to the wishes of others. Here of course, there is room for creativity, since there is constant conflict. It is at this level that neurotics remain, once they arrive.

The third stage is reached when all of our powers, working together, create an autonomous inner world in which we are at one with ourselves. Unfortunately, it is only the genius or extraordinary one among us who reaches this stage. As creative persons we evolve our ego ideal from ourselves. We develop standards which are beyond identification with the conventional superego morality and which are not based merely on the given but also on self-chosen factors, toward which we consciously strive.

Rank's mature thinking views the "will to immortality" as the key to our efforts to understand man. This "will to immortality" is our innate sense of connection with life and all its relationships, whether toward ourselves, others or God. A striving for self-perpetuation is inherent in human nature; it is the urge to maintain our individual identity beyond the limitatons of the body. We are in conflict with death, and while we cannot overcome it physically, we can do so "ideologically." Our will to live forever expresses itself and satisfies itself in terms of *belief*; and necessarily so, since the very nature of immortality prevents us from having definite

---

[44]Rank, *Will Therapy*, pp. 232, 263-64.

knowledge in advance, thus limiting us to an act of faith. While immortality belongs to the future, we work toward it in the present life through our attitudes and beliefs about it. Our striving toward it may take any one of a vast array of forms, including identifying with the group, believing in an indestructible soul, constructing a masterpiece and performing a heroic deed.[45]

If psychology is to fulfill its basic purpose, i.e., to enable us to find the meaning of our lives, it can do so only by guiding us to an experience "beyond psychology." The ultimate task of psychology is to re-establish our connection to life, bring us into personal touch with the sustaining and creative forces of life that are beyond intellectual doctrines and make these redemptive forces available to all. To live beyond psychology we must have a vital experience of our own — in religious terms, a revelation, conversion, or rebirth. Such an experience results in a sense of connection to life that extends beyond the present life. Immortality then becomes more than just continuing existence; it becomes personal participation in everlasting life. In this participation we find a "new soul" or experience "conversion."[46]

This conversion Rank calls[47] "life in Christ." Faith for it comes from the belief that Christ is actually living in us; the spirit of the resurrected Lord. This is a long step beyond psychological identification — a step *into identity*. Paul teaches that anyone who believes in the resurrected Jesus, will himself be resurrected, i.e., will have a new self such as he, Paul, had acquired. And such a resurrection, writes Rank just before his death, is the zenith of human experience.

A NEO-ANALYTIC WRITER

Erich Fromm

The issue of mental health is inseparable from the ultimate human problem, which is the achieving of the basic aims of

---

[45]Progoff, *Death and Rebirth*, pp. 230-32.
[46]*Ibid.*, pp. 250-51, 265.
[47]Rank, *Beyond Psychology*, pp. 150, 159.

life: independence, integrity and the ability to love. Our relationship to our environment is of basic importance to Fromm. He is highly critical of an "adjustment" concept in mental health. To be adjusted is to make ourselves into a commodity, where nothing is really stable about us except our need to please and our readiness to modify our role.[48]

To be able to love and to create, to be able to live intensely, to be fully born and fully awake; these are the aims of life. To fulfill them, we must emerge from "incestuous" family ties into the conviction of our real though limited strength. We must be able to accept the paradox that every one of us is *the most* important consideration in the universe. We are to love life, yet be able to accept death without terror. We must live by love, reason, and faith, and respect life, both our own and that of our fellowman.[49]

Fromm insists that the process of independence has two aspects:[50] first, we grow stronger physically, emotionally and mentally. As these spheres grow in intensity and activity, guided by our will and reason, they become more integrated. Self-strength increases within its social and individual limitations. Second, we experience a growing aloneness. Free from all the bonds that once gave meaning and security to life, we become isolated. Unable to bear the isolation we are driven to a new form of bondage, conformity, in which we gain security, but only at the sacrifice of integrity of the self. This aloneness is not inevitable, however. We can be free yet not alone, he says; independent yet an integral part of mankind. This freedom is to be attained by the realization of the total personality by the active expression of our potentialities. While these potentialities are present in all of us, they become real only as they are expressed spontaneously.

Fromm, like Rank, maintains[51] that while true spontaneity is a rare phenomenon, artists, philosophers, scientists and

[48]Fromm, *Psychoanalysis and Religion*, pp. 74-75.
[49]Fromm, *The Sane Society*, pp. 69, 203-04.
[50]Fromm, *Escape from Freedom*, pp. 29-30.
[51]*Ibid.*, pp. 259-61.

small children demonstrate its possibility. In fact, we all know persons who are or have been spontaneous, and most of us can observe at least moments of our own spontaneity. Rare though it may be, this spontaneity is the answer to the problem of freedom, for it is the one way in which we can overcome the terror of aloneness without sacrificing the integrity of our self; for in the spontaneous realization of the self we are united anew with the world, i.e., with others, nature and ourselves.

Love is the foremost component of spontaneity; not a love which is the dissolution of the self in another, nor the possession of another, but love as spontaneous affirmation of others and the union of ourselves with others for the purpose of preserving the individual self.[52] Love is primarily giving, not receiving. Genuine love is caring; it manifests itself in an active concern for the life and growth of that which we love. The affirmation of our life with its happiness, growth and freedom is rooted in our capacity to love.[53]

In addition to love, work is another component of spontaneity. Work, for Fromm, is not a compulsive activity to escape loneliness, nor an attempt to dominate nature, nor the worship of the products of our own hands; but work is that through which we become one with nature in the act of creation.[54]

By spontaneous self-realization and by relating ourselves to our world we avoid becoming isolated atoms. We become part of a structuralized whole; we have our rightful place, so that our doubts concerning ourselves and the meaning of life disappear. As we become aware of ourselves as active, creative persons, we recognize that there is but one meaning in life — the act of living itself. There is no higher power than this unique, individual self; we are the center and purpose of our life.[55]

---

[52]Ibid., p. 260.
[53]Fromm, The Art of Loving, pp. 18, 22, 50.
[54]Fromm, Escape from Freedom, p. 261.
[55]Ibid., pp. 262-65.

AN INDEPENDENT WRITER

Gordon Allport

Allport, one of America's leading psychologists, has made a careful study of the psychology of religion over many years. Religion has assumed a legitimate place in his human value structure. In the Study of Values Test (Allport, Vernon and Lindzey, 1960) religious values are included among the six basic motives in human personality along with economic, theoretical, aesthetic, social and political values.

Allport has pointed out[56] that psychotherapists, while recognizing the healing power of love, find themselves unable to do very much about it. By contrast, religion — and especially the Christian religion — offers an interpretation of life based wholly upon love (See I John 4:7-8). Although we rarely find a therapist who sees health-giving significance in the concept of the "love of God," many of us recognize the need of this love to make life seem complete, intelligible and right for us. Religion may be seen as superior to psychotherapy in the allowance it makes for the affiliative need in human nature.

The vocabularies of religion and modern science differ markedly. The religious vocabulary seems dignified but archaic, while the scientific vocabulary seems persuasive, but barbaric. Our id and superego have not learned to cooperate, observes the modern mental hygientist, while St. Paul expresses the same idea in these words: "The flesh lusteth against the Spirit, and the Spirit against the flesh" (Galatians 5:17, KJV). While there are differences in vocabulary, there are similar views regarding the origin, nature and cure for mental distress. Allport contends[57] that it is difficult to find any proposition in modern mental hygiene that has not been expressed in some portion of the world's great literature.

The attributes of Allport's mature personality are three

---

[56]Gordon Allport, *The Individual and His Religion.* (New York: The Macmillan Company, 1950), pp. 81-82.
[57]Allport, *The Individual*, p. 97.

in number.[58] First is the acquisition of a variety of psychogenic interests that center around ideal objects and values which are beyond the range of viscerogenic desire. Unless we can escape the level of immediate biological impulse our lives are substantially dwarfed and infantile. A second attribute is self-insightfulness, or the ability to objectify ourselves and to be reflective about our own lives. To possess such insight is to see ourselves as others see us, and at least occasionally to see ourselves in "cosmic perspective." The third is a unifying philosophy of life, which is not necessarily articulated, religious, or entirely complete. Without such a pattern, our lives seem fragmented and aimless. All strongly idealistic interests tend to be unifying elements in personality growth. The religious interest, however, being the most comprehensive, serves best as this vitally needed integrative agent. These three characteristics, self-expansion, self-objectification and self-unification, represent the three major avenues of development open to us in the course of our growth.

Psychotherapists and religionists are agreed that integration requires self-objectification, insight into our own value system and a clear picture of our assets and liabilities. Confession is a chief aid in such self-objectification. It is highly regrettable, and perplexing as well, from a psychological point of view, that such a valuable therapeutic technique has not been endorsed generally among Protestants.[59]

Since the process of becoming continues throughout life, it is only in the adult mind that we expect to find a fully-developed religious sentiment. Although our growing adult minds stretch their rational capacities to the limit, no matter how far they are extended, failure is inevitable. We *must* learn that, to surmount the difficulties of a cruel world, faith and love are indispensable.[60]

Allport defines the mature religious sentiment[61] as a dis-

[58]*Ibid.*, pp. 53, 92.
[59]*Ibid.*, pp. 95-97.
[60]Allport, *Becoming*, p. 95.
[61]Allport, *The Individual*, p. 56.

position, developed through experience, to respond favorably and habitually to conceptual objects and/or principles which we regard as both permanent or central as well as of supreme significance in our lives. Such a definition allows for maximum variation between persons as well as during the course of our individual growth. We must not expect that the religious sentiment, even when mature, will be completely consistent. More than other sentiments, its perfecting is always unfinished business.

The mature religious sentiment has six attributes.[62] First, it is well-differentiated; it has a richness, a complexity, and a multiplicity of interests that characterize it (such as, sentiment toward the church, toward the Divine, toward world brotherhood, toward good and evil, etc.). Second, it is dynamic in character; it is functionally autonomous, supplying its own driving power. Third, it is consistently effective in directing conduct. Fourth, it is comprehensive, including our emotions, values and strivings for perfection. Fifth, its design is integral and harmonious, and it gives freedom, for if we believe we are free we shall use our resources more flexibly than if we suppose we are in chains. Finally, it is "heuristic"; it stimulates further investigation; we hold to our beliefs until they can be substantiated or until we discover more valid ones.

To Allport, mental health is the *summum bonum* of life. It is through the insights of both religion and psychology that we can be expected to achieve our goal of facilitating mental health in human lives.

Selected Existentialists

Viktor Frankl

Frankl postulates a "will to meaning" that contrasts with, as well as builds upon, Freud's will to pleasure and Adler's "will to power." Just as the foundation for a house needs the superstructure before it becomes a building, so Psychoanalysis and Individual Psychology must be built upon if we

---

[62]*Ibid.*, pp. 57-74.

THE DYNAMICS OF WHOLENESS

are to have a concept of ourselves that is adequate for psychotherapy. Freud, Adler and Jung treat the spiritual dimension, which Frankl calls the essential characteristic of man,
in a totally inadequate manner. By reducing every human
experience to the psychological plane they have given us a
distorted view of ourselves. "Depth" psychology must give
way to "height" psychology to satisfy the "phenomenol-
ogical data of anthropological research."[63]

The writings of Frankl are dominated by the concept of
the meaningfulness of our existence, a concept tested for its
validity in the Nazi concentration camps of World War II.[64]
He was able to challenge his fellow prisoners contemplating
suicide there with the thought that life's great issue is not
what *we* expect from life, but, rather, what life is expecting
from us.

Belief in a super-meaning, whether as a metaphysical concept or as Providence, is of the foremost psychotherapeutic
and psychohygienic importance. Imbued with a genuine faith,
we gain creativeness and vitality, so that nothing in life appears meaningless or in vain.[65] Logotherapy focuses on the
meaning of human existence as well as on our search for
such a meaning. This striving to find meaning in life is the
primary motivating force within us.[66]

We do not act morally for the sake of having a good
conscience but for the sake of a cause to which we commit
ourselves. There is nothing in the world that will so effectively help us to survive even the worst conditions, as the
assurance of meaning in our lives.[67]

A person is an ego, not an id. We are not propelled by
an unconscious instinctive force, but by a spiritual unconscious. It is in this unconscious that our faith and religious
aspirations are grounded. When we come to God, it must

---

[63]Tweedie, *Logotherapy*, pp. 39-49.
[64]Frankl, *The Doctor and the Soul*, p. xi.
[65]*Ibid.*, p. 53.
[66]Frankl, *Man's Search*, p. 99.
[67]*Ibid.*, pp. 101-106.

be by spontaneous decision, not by having been driven.[68]
Values do not push a man, they pull him. To say we are
pulled by values is to imply freedom. Freedom for Frankl
is the choice between fulfilling a potentially meaningful situation or forfeiting it.[69]

Tension is inherent in human personality, and is indispensable to mental well-being. What we need is not a tension-
less state, but rather the striving and struggling for some
goal *worthy of us.* If an architect wants to strengthen a
decrepit arch, he increases the load which is laid on it, a process by which the parts are joined more firmly together.[70]

Frankl suggests three types of values through which we
find meaning in life.[71, 72] First, there are the values which
are realized in creative action: "creative" values, e.g., doing
a deed or engaging in a deliberate action such as helping
someone in need. The second set of values are "experiential" values; those which we realize in the experiences of life.
A work of nature or artistry that we enjoy, or the experience
of loving someone, exemplify this set of values.

Love is the only way we may grasp another human being
in the innermost core of his personality. By the spiritual
act of love, we are able to see the essential qualities as well
as the potential attributes of the loved one. Being a loving
person is to facilitate the actualization of these potentialities
in the other. By making him aware of what he can be and
what he should become, we cause these potentialities to become a reality.[73]

These creative and experiential values give meaning to life,
a meaning that is to be judged by the heights reached in
moments of intense experience. The height of a mountain
range is not measured by the height of some valley, but the
height of its tallest peak.[74]

---

[68]Tweedie, *Logotherapy,* p. 70.
[69]Frankl, *Man's Search,* p. 101.
[70]*Ibid.,* pp. 106-07.
[71]Arnold and Gasson, *The Human Person,* pp. 466-67.
[72]Frankl, *Man's Search,* pp. 113-15.
[73]Arnold and Gasson, *The Human Person,* pp. 472-73, 486.
[74]Frankl, *The Doctor,* p. 44.

THE DYNAMICS OF WHOLENESS

The third set of values is "attitudinal." The opportunity to realize attitudinal values is always present whenever we find ourselves confronted by a destiny toward which we can act only by acceptance. To realize attitudinal values is to "bear our cross," or manifest courage in suffering or dignity in doom and disaster. An inoperable cancer, e.g., might afford us our "last chance," so to speak, to actualize this supreme value of finding meaning in suffering.[75]

Frankl stresses the uniqueness and singularity of human personality. There is an implicit summons to actualize in our own lives our unique and singular possibilities. In all situations of life there is but one unique course by which we can realize our most personal potentialities; logotherapy would assist us in charting that course. Life is seen as an assignment; and we must ask, "What is expected of us?"[76]

The true meaning of life is found *in the world*, not within ourselves. The real aim of human existence, then, cannot be found in self-actualization. Human existence is instead, *self-transcendence*. Self-actualization is not a plausible aim at all for the more we would strive for it the more we would miss it. Only to the extent that we commit ourselves to the fulfillment of life's individual meaning for us can we actualize ourselves.[77]

Rollo May

Rollo May contends that the healthy person must effect a creative adjustment to God.[78] We would find ourselves in an impossible situation if it were not for "grace" (or clarification, for he uses these two terms interchangeably). Grace comes when, having suffered so much from the vicious cycle of egocentricity, we are willing to give up anything — our life, if need be. Fortunately, when we are ready to surrender, God is ready to come to our rescue! This surrender in no sense causes us to become static and unproductive, but brings

---

[75]*Ibid.*, p. 55.
[76]*Ibid.*, pp. 55-56, 58-59.
[77]Frankl, *Man's Search*, pp. 112-13.
[78]May, *The Art of Counseling*, pp. 219-22.

the most creative adjustment of tensions within; for our ego-centricity has been the major block to our creativity.

A sense of freedom overwhelms us following the experience of grace. Released from the unbearable conflict within, we are free to choose rightly. Our bondage to egocentricity and sin is in an important respect broken, and we can rejoice in our new liberation. We have at last found ourselves, our fellowman and our place in the universe. It is a transformation into personality health.[79]

Clarification, however, does not wipe the guilt away. But now we are able for the first time to accept and affirm our guilt. In fact, the very accepting of it in repentance is connected with the coming of grace. Guilt feeling, rather than being something morbid and shameful, is actually proof of our great possibilities and destiny.[80] We do not seek its elimination, then, but rather the transformation of neurotic guilt into normal guilt feelings, together with the capability of using these normal guilt feelings constructively.[81]

Because tensions remain, a new adjustment of tensions within the personality must be made. To be sure, when tensions are destructive, we may experience mental breakdown. But what we desire is the adjustment of tensions, not the escaping from them. We could not get rid of personality tensions even if this were desirable. We must have the courage to accept the necessity for having tensions and work out the most effective adjustment so that our personality will express itself most creatively.[82]

The source of personality problems is a lack of adjustment of tensions within the personality. The possibility of readjusting personality tensions, May claims, is nature's greatest gift to man! For it means growth, development and the fulfilling of our potentialities. Readjustment of personality tensions is synonymous with creativity.[83]

---

[79]*Ibid.*, pp. 223-24.
[80]*Ibid.*, pp. 74, 222.
[81]May, *Psychology and the Human Dilemma*, p. 109.
[82]May, *The Art of Counseling*, p. 30.
[83]*Ibid.*, p. 40.

Mental health is, in part, the capacity on the one hand to be aware of the gap between stimulus and response and, on the other, to use this gap constructively. Thus, mental health is on the opposite side of a continuum from "conditioning" and "control." The progress of therapy can be measured in terms of progress made in the "consciousness of freedom."[84]

One of the basic presuppositions of psychotherapy is that the patient must sooner or later accept the responsibility for himself.[85] Individuation is the "heightened awareness of the possibility of freedom," or what Kierkegaard calls the "alarming possibility of being able."[86] Consciousness of self actually expands the control of our lives, and with that expanded power comes the capacity to let ourselves go.

Freedom does not come automatically; we achieve it, not at a single bound, but each day. The basic secret in doing so is to choose ourselves, to affirm responsibility for ourselves, make our own decisions and fulfill our own destiny. This struggle for individuation necessitates a "cutting of the psychological umbilical cord." Unless it is cut, we remain like toddlers tied to a stake in our parents' front yard.[87]

Rollo May[88] doubts whether we really live until we have affirmed our own existence, that is, frankly confronted the terrifying fact that we could wipe out our own existence, but choose not to do so. When we choose consciously to live, two things happen. First, when we accept the responsibility for our own lives, not as a burden forced upon us but as something we have chosen ourselves, we become aware of personal responsibility and freedom. We exist as the result of a decision we have made. Second, discipline from the outside changes into self-discipline. We accept discipline because we have chosen what we want to do with our lives and the discipline is necessary for the sake of the values we wish to achieve.

---

[84]May, *Psychology and the Human Dilemma*, p. 174.
[85]May, *The Art of Counseling*, pp. 49, 51.
[86]May, *The Meaning of Anxiety*, p. 34.
[87]May, *Man's Search for Himself*, pp. 104-05, 144-45.
[88]*Ibid.*, pp. 146-49.

The neurotic's basic problem, as May analyzes it,[89] is an inability to affirm or trust. To affirm means more than simply to accept; it is *accepting actively;* it is saying, "Yes," not only mentally or verbally, but as a response of our entire personality. Not being able to trust, we lack confidence and courage. If we could have the power to trust and, with it, confidence and courage, we could give an affirmative answer to life and thus overcome it constructively. To trust more and to develop the courage of imperfection will cause a relaxation of our driving neurotic ambition and give our creative abilities a chance to find expression.

We are to affirm not only our relationships with God and ourselves, but our relationships to others as well. By cheerfully affirming our social responsibility and by expressing ourselves in socially constructive ways, we are able to "realize ourselves." As self-centered persons seeking to save our own lives, we lose them.[90]

Three important qualities play a significant role in our interpersonal relationships: love, empathy and appreciation. Rollo May, in his recent book, *Man's Search for Himself* (which he says might well have been entitled, *A Preface to Love*) defines love as a delight in the presence of the other individual, as an affirming of his worth and development to be equal with our own.[91]

Empathy, or "feeling into," which May calls the key to the counseling process, is that point where the psychic states of counselor and counselee merge. Outside the realm of counseling, no understanding is possible without empathy. Empathy is the fundamental process of love. Learning to empathize is relaxing mentally, spiritually and physically. It is the ability to let ourselves go into the other individual with a willingness to be changed in the process. Although it involves self-denunciation, through losing our personality tem-

[89]May, *The Art of Counseling,* pp. 141, 213-14.
[90]*Ibid.,* p. 66.
[91]May, *Man's Search for Himself,* pp. 204-06.

porarily we are able to find it "a hundred fold richer in the other person."[92]

A true relationship of understanding and appreciation of another person raises the prestige and sense of worth of the loved person. Such an understanding removes barriers separating us from our fellowman, drawing the other person for awhile out of his loneliness, welcoming him into community with another fellow human being.[93]

REPRESENTATIVE HUMANISTS

Carl Rogers

The humanistic writers' positive perspective on mental health is in strong contrast to that of the psychoanalysts (except Rank) and the objectivists with their tunnel vision of behavior.[94]

Carl Rogers sees human beings as having one fundamental need,[95] the tendency to actualize, support and enhance the organism. We maintain ourselves by assimilating food, behaving defensively in the face of threat, and, generally, by moving in the direction of maturation. We expand ourselves through growth and reproduction, always moving in the direction of greater independence. Finally, we actualize ourselves in the direction of socialization.

It is through struggle and pain that we move toward this enhancement and growth. Because the first steps in our learning to walk involve at least struggle and many times pain, we may revert to crawling for a time. But in the overwhelming majority of cases the forward direction of growth is more powerful than the rewards of remaining infantile. Similarly, we will become independent, responsible, self-governing and socialized. When we are given the opportunity for a clear-cut choice between progression and regression, the former invariably dominates.

---

[92]May, *The Art of Counseling*, p. 77, 97.

[93]*Ibid.*, p. 119.

[94]Carl Rogers, "Two Divergent Trends," in *Existential Psychology*, ed. by Rollo May. (New York: Random House, 1960), p. 87.

[95]Rogers, *Client-Centered Therapy*, pp. 487-91.

Self-actualization for Rogers is a natural unfolding similar to that found in other living things.[96] A by-product of this natural unfolding is that as we are more willing to be our-selves we find·that we are more willing to permit others to be themselves.[97]

In order to be self-actualized, first we must be integrated. Integration takes place when all the sensory and internal bodily experiences are admissible to consciousness through accurate symbolization, and are organizable into one consis-tent "structure of self." When this happens, our tendency toward growth can become fully operative, and we move in directions normal for all organic life.[98] Self-integration lib-erates energy that enables us to carry out actions to implement our reoriented striving toward life goals.[99]

Rogers admits to personal dissatisfaction over the com-monly-given answers regarding the prime purpose of life: to glorify God, to prepare for immortality, to satisfy every sensual desire, to achieve material possessions, or status, or knowledge, or power, or even to give ourselves unreservedly to a' cause outside of ourselves. His view of life's loftiest aim is expressed in the words of Kierkegaard: "To be that self which one truly is."[100]

Taking as his starting point trends observed in his own clients, Rogers maintains that to conceptualize our goals im-plies avoiding some common pressures or tendencies. For one thing, it means moving away from façades, from being selves that we are not. Also, it means refusing to be driven by the selves we "ought to be." Some of us have so internalized from our parents an "I-have-to-be-good" obsession that it is only after great struggle we can move away from this as a life-goal. Similarly, it means moving away from the com-

[96]Arnold and Gasson, *The Human Person*, p. 179.
[97]Rogers, *On Becoming a Person*, p. 327.
[98]Rogers, *Client-Centered Therapy*, pp. 513-14.
[99]Arnold and Gasson, *The Human Person*, p. 540.
[100]Soren Kierkegaard, "Fear and Trembling," *The Sickness Unto Death*, trans. by W. Lowrie, Anchor Books. (New York: Double-day, 1968), p. 29.

pulsion to meet the expectations of society (the "organization," the college, the group). By moving away from these, we are able to move toward Shakespeare's admonition: "To thine own self be true . . ."[101]

Our dominant goal is not just *away from* conformities, it is *toward self-direction*, in its many facets. First, we move in the direction of autonomy, toward choosing goals *we* consider worthy, toward deciding which activities have meaning for us and which do not. Second, we are not always "predictably consistent"; we do not invariably hold the same feelings toward experiences or other people. Third, we move toward an increasing openness to experience, i.e., a discovering of feelings and attitudes of which we previously have been unaware or unable to own as part of ourselves, progressively accepting them in a more affirming manner. Fourth, accepting our own experience, we are able to move toward the appreciation of the experiences of others. Fifth, we are able to place a basic trust in ourselves, to live by *personally* discovered values, and to express ourselves in our *own* unique ways. Finally, we are able to live spontaneously, to move toward an increasing tendency to live fully in each moment.[102]

The following statement[103] contains the essence of Rogers' "fully functioning person."

> It appears that the person who is psychologically free moves in the direction of becoming a more fully functioning person. He is more able to live fully in and with each and all of his feelings and reactions. He makes increasing use of all his organic equipment to sense, as accurately as possible, the existential situation within and without. . . . He is more able to permit his total organism to function freely in all its complexity in selecting, from the multitude of possibilities, that behavior which in this moment of time will be most generally and genuinely satisfying. He is able to put more trust in his organism

---

[101]Rogers, *On Becoming a Person*, pp. 164-70.
[102]*Ibid.*, pp. 170-75, 188.
[103]*Ibid.*, pp. 191-92.

in this functioning, not because it is infallible, but because he can be fully open to the consequences of each of his actions and correct them if they prove to be less than satisfying.

. . . He is his own sifter of evidence, and is more open to evidence from all sources, he is completely engaged in the process of being and becoming himself, and thus discover that he is soundly and realistically social; he lives more completely in this moment, but learns that this is the soundest living for all time.

Creativity for Rogers is the tendency to actualize ourselves and to become our potentialities. There are three inner aspects[104] of a creative act. First, we have an openness to and awareness of what exists at this moment, and are able to receive conflicting information without a compulsion to closure. (This openness is the exact opposite of psychological defensiveness.) Secondly, and perhaps most basic, we have an *internal* locus of evaluation. We have established the value of our product, it has the "feel of being me in action," of being an actualization of potentialities within. The last (and least) of the conditions of creativity is the ability to toy with elements, ideas, colors, shapes, relationships, to juggle them into impossible juxtapositions and to imagine wild hypotheses. Such activity sets the stage for the "hunch," the creative seeing of relationships in a new and significant way.

Abraham Maslow

A. H. Maslow, along with Erich Fromm, has been highly critical of adjustment as a goal of personality development, for it sets such a low ceiling upon our potentiality for growth. Even a cow, a slave, or a robot may be well-adjusted.[105] Maslow[106] upbraids psychology for its pessimistic, negativistic and highly limited conception of man. Focusing upon

[104]*Ibid.*, pp. 353-55.
[105]Maslow, *Motivation and Personality*, p. 376.
[106]Hall and Lindzey, *Theories of Personality*, p. 325.

our frailties and sins more than upon our strengths and virtues, psychology has voluntarily restricted itself to but half of its rightful jurisdiction, and that has been the darker and meaner half.

Each person's inner nature contains the "will to health." This "will to health" or urge to self-actualization is that which makes psychotherapy, education and self-improvement possible in principle.[107]

Maslow's theory of motivation assumes that needs are arranged along a hierarchy of priority or potency. When the needs having the greatest potency and priority are satisfied, the next needs in the hierarchy emerge and press for satisfaction, etc., up through the entire ladder of motives. The hierarchical order of motives from the most potent to the least potent is as follows: physiological needs, safety needs, needs for belongingness and love, esteem needs, needs for self-actualization, cognitive needs (such as thirst for knowledge) and aesthetic needs (such as the desire for beauty).

The need for a system of values is a cognitive need. A man needs, to quote Dr. Maslow:[108]

> A framework of values, a philosophy of life, a religion or religion-surrogate to live by and understand by, in about the same sense that he needs sunlight, calcium or love. This I have called the "cognitive need to understand." . . . Historically, we are in a value interregnum in which all externally given value systems have proven to be failures (political, economic, religious, etc.) e.g., nothing is worth dying for. What man needs but does not have, he seeks for unceasingly, and he becomes dangerously ready to jump at *any* hope, good or bad. The cure for this disease is obvious. We need a validated, usable system of human values that we can believe in and devote ourselves to (be willing to die for), because they are true rather than because we are exhorted to "believe and have faith." Such an empirically based *Weltanschauung* seems now to be a real possibility, at least in theoretical outline.

[107]Maslow, "Some Basic Propositions," pp. 35-36.
[108]*Ibid.*, pp. 42-43.

Maslow defines[109] the concept of self-actualization as the desire to become more and more what we are, and to become everything that we are capable of becoming. His extensive study of self-actualizing persons, that includes twenty-one public and/or historical figures and thirty contemporaries, reveals fifteen characteristics which distinguish such persons from others, namely their:

1) superior perception of reality;
2) increased acceptance of self, others and nature;
3) degree of spontaneity;
4) centering on problems (not on ego);
5) increased detachment and desire for privacy;
6) increased autonomy and independence;
7) freshness of appreciation and richness of emotional life;
8) mystical, spiritual and/or peak experiences;
9) increased identification with others;
10) profoundness of interpersonal relations;
11) democratic character structure;
12) increased ability to discriminate between means and ends;
13) philosophical, unhostile sense of humor;
14) increased creativeness;
15) resistance to enculturation.

A major difficulty with Maslow's earlier ideas about self-actualization is their somewhat static character. Observing "self-*actualization*" as an exclusive phenomenon among the older set (age 60 and above) he deduces a state of perfection, Nirvana, or "arrival." His more recent work emphasizes a "self-*actualizing*," a dynamic process of becoming that is perpetuated throughout our lives.[110]

---

[109]Maslow, *Motivation and Personality*, pp. 91-92, 199-234.
[110]Abraham H. Maslow, *Toward a Psychology of Being*, An Insight Book: (Princeton: D. VanNostrand Company, 1962), pp. 24, 42.

Maslow has noted[111] that while in principle growth toward self-actualization is relatively simple, it rarely happens in practice (by his own criteria, less than one per cent of the adult population). While there are doubtless many reasons for this, he lays primary blame upon the widespread conviction that our intrinsic nature is "evil," which carries the implication that we simply cannot rise above our own natures.

Among the objectively describable and measurable characteristics of his developing theory of the healthy human specimen, Maslow recently has identified these ten:[112]

1) a clearer, more accurate perception of reality;
2) an increased openness to experience;
3) an expanded integration, wholeness and unity;
4) a widening spontaneity and expressiveness; full functioning, aliveness;
5) a real self; a solid identity; autonomy; uniqueness;
6) an intensified objectivity and detachment;
7) a recovery and awareness of creativeness;
8) an ability to assimilate concreteness and abstractness;
9) a democratic character structure;
10) an ability to love.

Maslow contends[113] that we must achieve a transcendence of our environment by being independent of it, by being able to stand against it, fight it, neglect it, turn our back on it, refuse it or adapt to it. Practically all self-actualized persons, while superficially accepting conventional behavior, privately are casual, perfunctory and detached regarding it. They also

---

[111]Maslow, "Some Basic Propositions," p. 41.
    Note: For a more philosophical and extensive analysis of Maslow's theory of self-actualization, the serious reader is directed to *Perceiving, Behaving* and *Becoming*, prepared by the Association of Supervision and Curriculum Development (ASCD) as their 1962 Yearbook. Here Maslow develops 38 propositions, many of which bear directly upon mental health.
[112]Maslow, *Toward a Psychology of Being*, p. 148.
[113]*Ibid.*, pp. 169-72.

reveal a surprising amount of detachment from people, and a
strong liking — even a need — for privacy. This view provides a place for meditation, contemplation and other forms
of going into the self; of turning away from the outer world
to listen to the inner voices. Such a theory is much more
palatable now that we have accepted the fact that the unconscious contains certain kinds of truth, creativeness and love,
along with the shadowy and evil. Likewise, it is palatable
now that we are making a distinction between the coping (or
striving) aspect of behavior and the expressive (or effortless)
aspect, for expressive behaviors do not have as part of their
purpose adapting to environment.

Maslow expresses regret that the love need is ordinarily
studied as a deficit need, as an emptiness which has to be
filled. Healthy persons among us need little love; steady,
small, "maintenance" doses are sufficient, and they may be
without even these for periods of time. Clinical studies of
healthy persons show that although they have less need to
receive love, they are more able to give love, and are thus
more "loving" people.[114]

In his enlightening chapter on love in self-actualized persons, Maslow discusses several important facets of love.[115]
First, self-actualized persons tend toward an increasing spontaneity, resulting in the dropping of pretenses, roles and strivings in the love relationship. In such a union, it is not necessary to impress, suppress or repress. They can be themselves
without feeling there are demands or expectations placed
upon them. Second, such persons usually possess the ability
to love and to be loved. Third, sex and love are usually fused
in healthy people. Love and sex satisfactions both improve
with the age of the relationship. Such people do not need
sensuality, but they enjoy it wholeheartedly when it occurs.
Fourth, erotic and agapean love, though different, merge in
the healthiest people. While in the general public, they appear
to be at opposite poles, in self-actualizing people the dichot-

[114]*Ibid.*, p. 39.
[115]Maslow, *Motivation and Personality*, pp. 238-60.

omies are resolved; they are at the same time selfish and unselfish, active and passive, masculine and feminine, etc.

Fifth, self-actualized persons experience "need identification"; they feel others' needs as if they were their own. Sixth,
fun, merriment, elation and a feeling of well-being characterize these subjects: they can enjoy themselves in love and
sex. Seventh, self-actualized persons affirm others' individuality and unique personality. Such persons are pleased rather
than threatened by others' triumphs. Eighth, their love is a
spontaneous admiration, a sort of receptive and undemanding
awe and enjoyment such as that experienced when one is
"struck" by a fine painting.

Creativeness for Maslow[116] cannot be distinguished from
our essential humanness, and in effect is synonymous with
health itself. Self-actualized creativity is emitted like radio-
activity; it hits all of life in a similar manner to a radiant individual's cheerfulness, which emanates without purpose or
even consciousness.

Somewhat related are peak experiences, i.e., those experiences that bring us closest to identity, or *are our identity*.
Maslow enumerates a number of facets of peak experiences.[117]
First, we feel more integrated, unified, or "whole" than at
other times. Also we become more purely ourselves; we are
more able to fuse with the world and with what has been
"non-self." We feel ourselves to be *the* responsible person; like a prime mover, more self-determined; more "our
own boss"; with more "free will" than at other times.
Similarly, we are at such times most free of inhibitions,
cautions and fears. On the positive side, we are more spontaneous and expressive, more innocently naive and honest,
more natural and unrestrained. We are more creative and
improvising, and more impromptu and novel.

In the peak experience we reach our acme of uniqueness
and individuality, and we are the most "here-now," the most
free of the past and the future. We become more a pure
psyche and less a "pawn-of-the-world"; we become more

---

[116]Maslow, *Toward a Psychology of Being*, pp. 136-37.
[117]*Ibid.*, pp. 97-108.

non-striving and non-needing, for joy has been attained. Our expression and communication may become poetic and rhapsodic. We experience total discharge, catharsis, culmination, or consummation. We are ourselves, experiencing a certain completion or even perfection. Feelings of playfulness, exuberance and delight abound.

We feel lucky, fortunate, or graced. Thus we are often overwhelmed by gratitude to God (if we are religious), or anything and everything that has helped to make this wonder possible. Frequently this feeling of gratitude leads to an all-embracing love for everyone and everything, to a perception of the world as beautiful and good; even to a sense of obligation and an eagerness to repay.

Peak times are moves toward health and are themselves "momentary healths." They are integrative of the conflicts between us and other persons, or within us, or between us and the world. Finally, they are life-validating; i.e., they make life worthwhile.[118]

In a peak experience we take on, temporarily, many of the characteristics of the self-actualized person. These are not only our happiest and most thrilling moments, they are our healthiest moments, the moments of greatest maturity, individuation and fulfillment.

Such episodes can, theoretically, come any time in life to any person. What seems to distinguish self-actualizing people is that to them the episodes seem to come far more frequently and intensely than in others.[119]

Maslow would have us re-define self-actualization, then, in such a way as to take away its static and typological shortcomings and make it less an all-or-nothing affair, into which a few rare individuals enter around age sixty.[120] It is an episode in which our powers come together in an especially efficient and enjoyable way, whereby we are more integrated, more open to experience, more expressive and spontaneous, more fully functioning, creative and ego-transcending, and

---

[118]Maslow, "Some Basic Propositions," p. 45.
[119]Maslow, *Toward a Psychology of Being*, p. 91.
[120]*Ibid*.

more independent of lower-level needs. In such episodes we become more truly ourselves, more perfectly actualizing our own potentialities and more closely resembling the inner core of our being.

A Christian Perspective of Health

Health is confident surrender. Healthy Christians are characterized by a heightened awareness of a sense of belongingness to God. Such an awareness, E. Stanley Jones maintains, shifts our focus from the egocentric to the Christocentric. We are not called to get to heaven, nor to be holy, nor happy nor even to serve God; we are called to *belong* to Jesus Christ (Romans 1:6). To *be* centers on self; to *belong* centers on Christ.[121] When the decision is made to surrender to Christ and make Him the center, then everything belongs to Him.

The awareness of Christ-centeredness is perpetuated as long as we remain abandoned to Him. Hear the Apostle Paul (Romans 8:35-39), Phillips) as he asks:

> Who can separate us from the love of Christ? Can trouble, pain or persecution? Can . . . danger to life and limb . . . ? No, in all these things we win an overwhelming victory through him who has proved his love for us.
>
> I have become absolutely convinced that neither death nor life, neither messenger of Heaven nor monarch of earth, neither what happens today nor what may happen tomorrow, neither a power from on high nor a power from below, nor anything else in God's whole world has any power to separate us from the love of God in Christ Jesus our Lord!

This surrender is not tentative; it is decisive, once and for all. There is a daily surrender of things, before unknown, which keep coming up; but that is different from the central surrender, which is permanent.[122] To continue to belong is to maintain the surrendered life. The decisive surrender to

---

[121]E. Stanley Jones, *The Way to Power and Poise* (New York: Abingdon Press, 1949), p. 75.
[122]*Ibid.*

Christ means a transition from an "eccentric" life integrated around the ego-image, to a well-centered life pivoting around the self in Christ.[123]

This continuous "giving up" does not mean a renouncing of creativity. On the contrary, Rollo May assures us,[124] grace brings about the most creative adjustment of the tensions within the personality. Our egocentricity has been the blockage to our creativity. Freed from it, we are able to express that creativity much more directly, spontaneously and gratifyingly. The creativity of grace, then, frees us from having to waste our energies struggling against inhibitions, constrictions, and other hindrances which our egocentricity was placing in our way.

Health is transparent spontaneity. Continuing consciousness of relationship requires open and relaxed surrender in all of the moral struggles. An attitude of honesty and openness facilitates a confession to whatever lack of surrender, failure and continuing selfishness we see in ourselves. Concealment of sin, hostility and selfishness conversely only serve to erect a barrier and push us toward hypocrisy. To be able to acknowledge, without shame, the broader range of our real selves is a vital factor in maintaining health.[125]

"It is not until we *are* our real selves and *act* our real selves that our real selves are in a postion to grow," says Jourard.[126] As we are transparent with ourselves, spontaneity becomes possible. This spontaneity enables us to choose and express our feelings, and frees us from the compulsion to "play games," to use Eric Berne's phrase,[127] and have only the feelings we have been taught. In the spontaneous realization of the self we unite ourselves anew with the world and

---

[123]Fritz Kunkel, *In Search of Maturity* (New York: Charles Scribner's Sons, 1949), pp. 220-21.

[124]May, *The Art of Counseling*, pp. 221-22.

[125]Sidney Jourard, *The Transparent Self*, An Insight Book. (Princeton: D. VanNostrand Company, 1964), p. 105.

[126]*Ibid.*, p. 25.

[127]Eric Berne, *Games People Play* (New York: Grove Press, 1964), p. 180.

ourselves. Love is the foremost component of that spontaneity.[128]

Spontaneity is living for today in day-tight compartments,
shutting off yesterday and tomorrow.[129] We pray, "Give us
this day our daily bread" (Matthew 6:11) and exclaim with
the Psalmist, "This is the day which the Lord has made; let
us rejoice and be glad in it" (Psalm 118:24).

We long for the kind of spontaneity of Zorba the Greek,[130]
whose love for life and spontaneity led him to affirm every
aspect of his being.

> I've stopped thinking all the time of what happened yes-
> terday. And stopped asking myself what's going to happen
> tomorrow. What's happening today, this minute, that's
> what I care about. I say, "What are you doing at this
> moment, Zorba?" "I'm sleeping." "Well, sleep well."
> "What are you doing at this moment, Zorba?" "I'm work-
> ing." "Well, work well." "What are you doing at this
> moment, Zorba?" "I'm kissing a woman." "Well, kiss her
> well, Zorba. And forget all the rest while you're doing
> it; there's nothing else on earth, only you and her! Get
> on with it!"

By depending on God we are free of men, things and self,
free to be able to take pleasure in all His gifts, without being
the slave of any.[131] Our spontaneity in the spirit of loving
obedience allows us to adopt Augustine's admonition: "Love
God and do what you will." We will not permit the world
to squeeze us into its mold, but determine instead to "let God
remould [our] minds from within, so that [we] may prove
in practice that the plan of God for [us] is good, . . . and
moves toward the goal of true maturity" (Romans 12:2,
Phillips).

---

[128]Fromm, *Escape from Freedom*, pp. 258-61.
[129]Dale Carnegie, *How to Stop Worrying and Start Living* (New
York: Simon and Schuster, 1948), p. 3.
[130]Nikos Kazantzakis, *Zorba the Greek*, trans. by Carl Wildman.
(New York: Simon and Schuster, 1953), p. 273.
[131]May, *The Art of Counseling*, pp. 227-28.

Health is purposeful integration. The healthy personality is an integrated whole, a basic unity in which the body, soul and spirit are integrated. Psychology's chief contribution to mental health, says Gordon Allport, is its concept of single-mindedness and integration.[132] St. Paul urges us to "attain to the unity of the faith" (Ephesians 4:13). Gandhi is said to have been mentally healthy because in him word, creed and deed were one; he was integrated.[133]

If our personality is to attain to its full expansion, we must be progressing toward the development of all of our potentialities into a harmonious unity.[134] This central striving for wholeness or perfection confers unity upon the personality. Adler is credited with being the first of the personality theorists to see striving for perfection or superiority as the great upward drive.[135] Every other drive receives its power from the striving for completion. Jung concurs that self-actualization is the goal of psychic development. Rogers and Goldstein likewise insist that the organism has a single goal; to strive, actualize, enhance and maintain itself.[136] For Rank, personality completion is not so much a striving as a freedom to strengthen and enhance our own personality. The aim of will therapy is "self-development," developing ourselves into that which we are.[137] Implied in all of these theories is that man's chief end is to glorify himself and to enjoy himself.

Frankl has declared that meaningfulness is to be found in the realm of values: creative values, e.g., doing a deed; experiential values, realized in the enjoyment of a concert or the joy of a friendship; and attitudinal values, e.g., displaying

---

[132]Allport, *The Individual and His Religion*, p. 92.

[133]Louis Fischer, "Gandhi's 'Soul Force'," in *Morality and Mental Health*, ed. by O. Hobart Mowrer. (Chicago: Rand McNally and Company, 1967), p. 623.

[134]Hostie, *Religion and the Psychology of Jung*, p. 70.

[135]Hall and Lindzey, *Theories of Personality*, p. 120.

[136]Melvin H. Marx and William A. Hillix, *Systems and Theories in Psychology* (New York: McGraw-Hill Book Company, 1963), p. 340.

[137]Rank, *Will Therapy*, p. 228.

courage and patience under adverse conditions.[138] As we comprehend the insights of Frankl we see that we must go beyond self-development and self-actualization. The central tenet of logotherapy is that our personality is integrated as we find meaning in our own lives — through the achieving of a set of values outside of ourselves. We must be challenged by a self-transcendent cause — a cause worthy of us — to find the fulfillment of life's meaning for us.[139] If Mr. Facing-both-ways ever becomes Mr. Facing-one-way, Fosdick observes, faith in some person, cause or idea believed in as worthwhile and surrendered to as worth serving, has inevitably played a part.[140] Rees notes[141] that to be captured by Christ is to be made a "this-one-thing-I-do" man.

The goal we as integrated Christians strive for is not *something*, but *Someone,* whose perfection we gradually make our own.[142] Such a goal takes us "beyond psychology." Psychology's road leads to *self*-fulfillment, *self*-enhancement and *self*-actualization. Social interrelationships, while frequently emphasized, are primarily means by which the individual enhances himself. God-consciousness is rarely stressed, and we see the goals for what they are — *self-glorification* and *self-obsession.* The Christian path leads beyond psychology, it is a path that features a striving to be like Him, and a going beyond ourselves, redemptively, in the affirmation of others.

Health is adjusting tension. Frankl suggests[143] that a search for meaning may arouse inner tension, rather than bringing equilibrium. Tension is an indispensable prerequisite for mental health; it is the gap between what we have already achieved and what we still ought to accomplish.

God's grace effects a creative adjustment of tensions be-

---

[138]Arnold and Gasson, *The Human Person,* pp. 466-67.
[139]Frankl, *Man's Search for Meaning,* p. 107.
[140]Fosdick, *On Being a Real Person,* p. 239.
[141]Paul S. Rees, *The Adequate Man,* (Westwood, New Jersey: Fleming H. Revell Company, 1959), p. 83.
[142]Arnold and Gasson, *The Human Person,* p. 179.
[143]Frankl, *Man's Search for Meaning,* p. 106.

tween the self which we are and the "ideal self" which we ought to be. The concept of equilibrium or balance as the goal of mental health is misleading and static. The possibility of readjusting personality tensions is nature's greatest gift to us. Our challenge is to recognize personality tension and conflict as potentially creative.[144]

While the central striving for wholeness confers unity upon man, it is never the unity of fulfillment or eliminated tension.[145] Perfect integration is never achieved; the mature religious sentiment is never completely consistent; it is always incomplete.[146]

Integration is an affair of psychological government, with all of the recurrent dissents, pressures and revolts to which government, regardless of however united and strong it may be, is subject. Integration is often hindered, psychologists agree, by grimly determined effort. We cannot blow on our hands, put our backs into it, and *will* peace of mind, purity of heart or freedom from bitterness.[147] Psychiatrists of the Nancy school have noted that often the effort to keep from doing something wrong seems to magnify the chances of performing that very act.[148] Closely related is the observation of St. Paul: "I find it to be a law that when I want to do right, evil lies close at hand" (Romans 7:21).

We must not make the mistake of affirming only what is good in ourselves, or affirming the universe only as long as it is good to us.[149] Tournier observes that what may appear to be detrimental may well be creative. The purpose of the gardener in pruning his vine is that it will bear fruit; it is not to restrict life, but to promote its fuller and richer flow.[150]

Accepting the challenge of tension and imbued with a

---

[144]May, *The Art of Counseling*, pp. 69, 221.

[145]Allport, *Becoming*, p. 67.

[146]Allport, *The Individual and His Religion*, p. 93.

[147]Fosdick, *On Being a Real Person*, pp. 45, 215.

[148]Allport, *The Individual and His Religion*, p. 93.

[149]*Ibid.*, p. 223.

[150]Paul Tournier, *The Meaning of Persons* (New York: Harper and Brothers, 1957), p. 227.

knowledge of our strengths and weaknesses, we are to set
forth confidently to eliminate and sublimate our weaknesses
and to increase and capitalize upon our strengths. Maturity
comes when, in creative conflict, we overcome our sins, frustrations, sickness, tragedy and deprivation. Faith in our ultimate triumph over life's circumstances brings a unity that
transforms destructive conflicts into constructive ones.

Suffering is among the most potentially creative forces in
nature, for it makes possible the fulfillment of attitudinal values and an inner growth. "It is under the blows of fate,"
Frankl observes, "in the white heat of suffering, that life is
hammered and formed."[151] Jung argues[152] that creativeness in the spiritual realm as well as every psychic advance
we make comes about because of mental suffering.

Christians are to *rejoice* in suffering, realizing that every
moment of suffering is an opportunity for growth. The
Scriptures underscore this truth repeatedly. I Peter 4:13,
KJV, admonishes: "Rejoice, inasmuch as ye are partakers of
Christ's sufferings." "Ye shall have tribulation; but be of
good cheer," advises John 16:33, KJV. Paul exults: "We
rejoice in our sufferings" (Romans 5:3).

Courageously, then, we affirm temptation, tension and suffering. While we shall doubtless stumble and fall in the midst
of temptation, we pick ourselves up quickly. "I am writing
this to you," John says, "so that you may not sin; but if any
one does sin, we have an advocate with the Father, Jesus
Christ the righteous" (I John 2:1). David Levy contends
that one of the hallmarks of good emotional health is resil-
iency and bounce.[153]

Health is wholehearted affirmation. Affirmation is a dy-
namically positive attitude by which we constantly authenti-
cate the whole process of living. To affirm life is to set
free our creative abilities. William James challenges us, "Believe that you possess significant reserves of energy and en-

[151]Frankl, *The Doctor*, p. 111.
[152]Jung, *Modern Man in Search of a Soul*, p. 260.
[153]Mowrer, *The Crisis in Psychiatry and Religion*, p. 91.

durance and your belief will create the fact."[154] Norman Vincent Peale[155] contends that if we change our thoughts we will change our world.

We are to affirm all of life as sacred — that "in everything God works for good with those who love him" (Romans 8:28). Our inevitable guilt feelings and tensions are to be affirmed creatively; not just accepted or tolerated; but used as stepping stones on a path that can lead from victory unto victory.

To affirm life is to affirm our own adequacy. E. Stanley Jones concedes that we know little about being able to step up to life, with its many demands, humbly conscious that we have within us a mastery that is able to face the business of living with adequacy. Paul Rees points to the Apostle Paul as the embodiment of that amazing adequacy for life in all of its circumstances, an adequacy that comes through attachment to the "Adequate One."[156] Thus could Paul declare: "I can do all things in him who strengthens me," and assure the Philippian church members, "My God will supply every need of yours according to his riches in glory in Christ Jesus" (Philippians 4:13, 4:19). We are to acknowledge our inadequacy, as well; for God's answer to Paul's request for deliverance from his infirmity was, "My grace is enough for you: for where there is weakness, my power is shown the more completely" (II Corinthians 12:9, Phillips).

The structure of spiritual wholeness rests upon the principle of "three-way" love: upper, outer, and inner; love for God, for others and for self. Mowrer cleverly ties these three together: "I tried to find myself and tried to find my God. But then I sought my brother and then I found all three." The relationships of the fully integrated person, says Rollo May, are characterized by affirmation toward God and the cosmos (*Umwelt*), toward one's fellowman (*Mitwelt*) and toward

---

[154]Norman Vincent Peale, "Picture It," *Guideposts*, May, 1967, p. 22.

[155]Norman Vincent Peale, *A Guide to Confident Living* (New York: Prentice-Hall, 1948), p. 181.

[156]Rees, *The Adequate Man*, pp. 99-100.

himself (*Eigenwelt*).[157] The self-actualized person of Maslow's study is able to affirm himself, others and nature.[158]

A lawyer, engaging Christ in conversation, asks: "Which is the great commandment in the law?" He replies,

> You shall love the Lord your God with all your heart, and with all your soul, and with all your mind. This is the great and first commandment. And a second is like it, You shall love your neighbor as yourself. On these two commandments depend all the law and the prophets.

The meaning of life is fulfilled through love. "Beloved, let us love one another; for love is of God, and he who loves is born of God, and knows God. He who does not love does not know God; for God is love" (Matthew 22:36-40; I John 4:7-8).

Affirmation of ourselves finds an appropriate balance in an adequate affirmation of God and others. It is easy to go too far in the matter of loving ourselves as well as not far enough. Fromm, in his affirmation of the uniqueness of the self, overreaches in maintaining that we are the center and purpose of our lives, and that growth and autonomy can never be subordinated to purposes that supposedly have greater dignity.[159] Liebman's admonition[160] follows a similar pattern: we are to love ourselves before squandering it on others.

The extreme of too little self-love is represented by such phrases as "worm of the dust" or the verse:

> Oh to be nothing,
> Just to lie at His feet,
> A broken and empty vessel,
> For the Master's use made meet.

In Christianity, we are heightened and affirmed, not destroyed and made "self-less." Christ takes "nobodies," and

---

[157]May, Angel and Ellenberger, eds., *Existence*, p. 54.

[158]Maslow, *Motivation and Personality*, p. 206.

[159]Fromm, *Escape from Freedom*, p. 265.

[160]Liebman, *Peace of Mind*, p. 39.

makes "somebodies."[161] "Love your neighbor *as yourself*" implies respect for our own integrity and uniqueness. Love for others and love for ourselves are not alternatives. On the contrary, a disposition of love toward ourselves is to be found in all who are capable of loving others.[162]

To really live, we must have a wholesome and realistic self-estimation, a sense of our own uniqueness. We cannot believe ourselves to be in the image of God, deeply and sincerely, with full conviction, and not receive a new source of strength and power.[163] To gain our balance in this area is to comprehend Christ's "second" commandment: "You shall love your neighbor as yourself" (Matthew 22:39).

We are to become increasingly aware of the needs of others, and able to regard them as persons rather than as objects to be used for our own selfish ends. We live by and through relationships; we become the self through "linkages with the non-self." An ungiven self is an unfulfilled self. Our constant task, says Overstreet, is to link ourselves in joy and contribution to all the life-giving movements of our world.[164]

To find ourselves means discovering unlimited growth potential, toward individual creativity, expanding brotherhood and spiritual empowering. Mature persons while free, independent and self-responsible on the one hand, become, on the other hand, an increasingly integral part of the total group. The more mature we become, the more we realize our dependence.[165]

As we become what Rogers calls fully functioning persons,[166] we become increasingly willing for others to become or to be themselves. By being open and transparent with others, we are able, for the first time, to become open

[161]Jones, *The Way to Power and Poise*, p. 74.
[162]Fromm, *The Art of Loving*, pp. 49-50.
[163]Maxwell Maltz, *Psycho-Cybernetics*, Wilshire Book. (Hollywood: Wilshire Book Company, 1960), p. 245.
[164]Overstreet, *The Mature Mind*, pp. 71, 268.
[165]Kunkel, *In Search of Maturity*, pp. 191-93.
[166]Rogers, *On Becoming a Person*, pp. 194, 327.

to ourselves. In fact, Jourard postulates[167] that we cannot come to know ourselves except through disclosing ourselves to another.

Love accepts others just as they are, as unique persons, while seeing them in terms of what they can be or will be. Requited love is creative; it helps the beloved to actualize those values which the lover sees as potentiality. Wanting to resemble the picture the beloved has of him, the lover in turn will strive to become more and more "what the lover and God intended and wanted him to be."[168]

St. Paul's depth of insight and height of oratory incomparably proclaim the eternal value and centrality of love. Not only is love the greatest human value, he declares, but other achievements, however Christian they may appear, are as nothing without love (I Corinthians 13).

Since Adler wrote that all human failures spring from a lack of love, hardly a psychologist since has not addressed himself to the vital subject of love, and rightly so. To be capable of giving and receiving love is the soundest criterion of fulfilled persons.[169] What theologians call agape love is the universal solution to conflict within man, as well as between men.[170] No wonder Maslow is insistent that we *must* understand love, we *must* be able to teach it, to create it, to predict it, or else the world is lost to hostility and suspicion.[171]

Health is appropriating resources. To affirm the Divine within is to begin appropriating His resources. To name even a few of them is to be staggered over the implications of our potentialities: love, compassion, power, freedom, forgiveness, soundness of mind, hope, faith, peace, joy, courage, grace, overcoming of temptation. Power, e.g., is not a matter of self-generation, Fosdick reminds us,[172] but of ap-

---

[167]Jourard, *The Transparent Self*, pp. 185-86.
[168]Arnold and Gasson, *The Human Person*, p. 473.
[169]Overstreet, *The Mature Mind*, p. 102.
[170]Tweedie, *The Christian and the Couch*, p. 192.
[171]Maslow, *Motivation and Personality*, p. 236.
[172]Fosdick, *On Being a Real Person*, pp. 214, 216.

propriation. Some of us are like self-contained pools. We have so much resource and no more. Expenditure threatens depletion. Others of us are like rivers; there is plenty of water available. In such cases the power does not originate in us, but flows through us.

Christ's example and teachings assure us that the resources for abundant living are available. His life was like a well, and from deeper sources than His own came a constant supply of appropriated power.[173] Out of the believer's heart "shall flow rivers of living water" (John 7:38). He challenges us:

> Whoever says to this mountain, 'Be taken up and cast into the sea,' and does not doubt in his heart, but believes that what he says will come to pass, it will be done for him. Therefore . . . whatever you ask in prayer, believe that you receive it, and you will (Mark 11:23-24).

Through faith in God, whose supply of resources is limitless, we are able to appropriate all the inner resources we need through faith and prayer. Faith, initially, is the decision to stake our whole existence on the person and work of Jesus Christ. Perpetuated, it is an inner act of confidence and commitment that naturally integrates us around the object of that faith. As such it is of the greatest significance for psychological health. Rooted in inner strength, faith makes us strong.

Through prayer, we feel a release of new life which renews our entire being. It is thus that we discover our personal, true feelings, our aspirations and convictions.[174] When we pray, Alexis Carrel, world-renowned scientist, writes,[175]

> We link ourselves with the inexhaustible motive power that spins the universe. We ask that a part of that power be apportioned to our needs. Even in asking, our human

[173]*Ibid.,* p. 219.
[174]Tournier, *The Meaning of Persons,* p. 224.
[175]Alexis Carrel, "Prayer is Power," *The Readers' Digest,* March, 1941, p. 35.

deficiencies are filled and we arise strengthened and repaired.

Health is resource investment. The Christian life is a balance between prayer and action, Tournier[176] reasons; between the dialogue in which we seek creative inspiration and the bold and confident affirmation of self in which we put into practice the inspiration received. While he admits this enterprise is difficult if not impossible, it is nevertheless that which creates us as persons, and which is the source from which new life and freedom spring.

The "action" side of investment includes good works, according to Christ and St. Paul. "Let your light so shine before men, that they may see your good works," Jesus said, "and give glory to your Father who is in heaven" (Matthew 5:16). All Scripture is given, "that the man who belongs to God may be efficient and equipped for good work of every kind" (II Timothy 3:17, NEB).

Psychologists have long recognized the value of work in helping us forget ourselves and become less egocentric. They have acknowledged likewise that work provides an opportunity for actualizing creative values, through the unique manner in which we approach it. Both Frankl and Rank have caught the essence of the potential that work may contribute to our spiritual wholeness. Frankl contends that the self is truly enhanced only when it is directed away from itself, when e.g., it creates through work or when it actualizes itself by sharing with others in love.[177] Rank declares that if we are working to realize our creativity or to contribute something outstanding to art, science or business, our strivings for immortality by such means are selfish strivings. He urges us to go beyond such a limited concept to a realization of work as a spiritual experience through which we find both a "new soul" and an "intimate connection to life."[178] The spiritual man is on an even higher road where the supreme ad-

---

[176]Tournier, *The Meaning of Persons,* p. 227.
[177]Arnold and Gasson, *The Human Person,* pp. 470, 486.
[178]Progoff, *The Death and Rebirth of Psychology,* pp. 247, 251-52.

venture is to experience the love of God in Jesus Christ and transmit it to others.

Man's full affirmation, then, is expressed in investment. Such an investment is diverse (time, talent, and possessions) and comprehensive; our total selves are given unstintingly to the lives of others. To relate redemptively to others is to release the resources of God in their direction; to be a channel of God's grace to those within the sphere of our influence.

Christianity at its highest and best is the appropriating of God's resources in behalf of our fellowman in need. We are to be instruments through which Christ can accomplish His work and His will in the world. Frank Laubach pictures graphically how we can become this channel: we are to throw one arm up vertically to receive Christ's love and throw the other arm out horizontally to channel it.[179] In this way, our lives become an investment in the lives of others, to the glory of Christ.

Summary

We need as a part of our Christian perspective a model of Christian growth; one that takes into consideration such factors as the birth experience, growth, conflict, direction, growth fluctuations, alternatives to the life of the Spirit, and an ideal of the Spirit-filled life.

In life's developmental process, we move through four stages: birth, childhood, adolescence and adulthood. In normal development, we pass from one to another of these stages with some disequilibrium, of course, but in general, relatively smoothly.

In our model of Christian growth and development we postulate the same four levels of development: the "new birth," a secure childhood, a conflict-ridden adolescence and spiritual maturity.

Life in Christ begins with a birth experience. This "new birth" is attended by pain and suffering; it comes about

---

[179]Bruce Larson, *Dare to Live Now!*, Zondervan Books. (Grand Rapids: Zondervan Publishing House, 1965), pp. 42-43.

THE DYNAMICS OF WHOLENESS

by confession of our sins, commitment of our total being to God, and faith that God honors that commitment.

This radical transformation of the personality is a miracle brought about by the grace of God. "If a man is in Christ he becomes a new person altogether — the past is finished and gone, everything has become fresh and new" (II Corinthians 5:17, Phillips). We have passed from egocentricity to object-centricity; i.e., from self-obsession to Christ-obsession. It is only through Christ that spiritual wholeness can exist. True health must have this radical beginning.

The healing of the soul requires Divine major surgery, operating upon the sinful life and nature of the individual. Because it is so radical, it is painful. But pain is as essential in spiritual birth as it is in physical birth.

Confession, restitution and repentance are painful experiences. And, generally, they are preceded by deep despair, loneliness, frustration, and meaninglessness or disillusionment with life. But when the final surrender is made we emerge triumphantly, and a new life has begun.

Psychology can take us only so far along this path. The radical transformation we have been describing here is not something accomplished by human effort or a new set of attitudes. It is the power of God working in our lives at the point of our confession, submission and faith. This experience, variously called conversion, salvation and the "new birth," is not an escape from the realities of life nor a tool of the church; it is a *profound human necessity*, a prelude to the achievement of true healthiness of personality. It is the needed plus factor that gives meaning, direction, zest and power for living.

Once the Divine encounter has been made, we are ready for life. This life in Christ follows three stages: childhood, adolescence and adulthood.

The childhood stage of Christian living is characterized by growth, security, spontaneity, and conformity. We accept the teachings of authority (specifically parents and church) without question. We are living in the "awe" stage of our relationship to God, and our obedience follows a rather easy,

A MODEL OF CHRISTIAN GROWTH

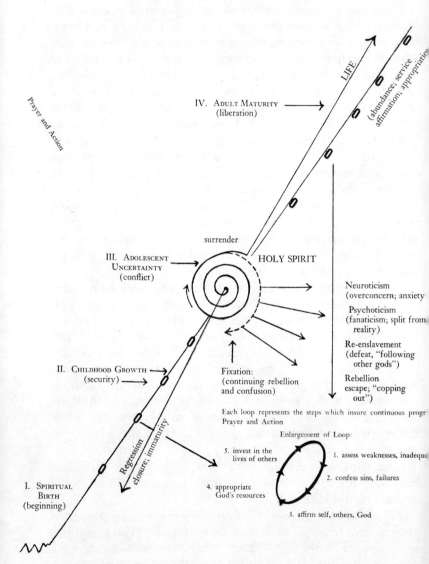

LIFE

(abundance; service affirmation; appropriatio[n])

Prayer and Action

IV. ADULT MATURITY
(liberation)

surrender

III. ADOLESCENT
UNCERTAINTY
(conflict)

HOLY SPIRIT

Neuroticism
(overconcern; anxiety)

Psychoticism
(fanaticism; split from
reality)

Re-enslavement
(defeat, "following
other gods")

II. CHILDHOOD GROWTH
(security)

Fixation:
(continuing rebellion
and confusion)

Rebellion
escape; "copping
out")

Each loop represents the steps which insure continuous progr[ess]
Prayer and Action

Regression
closure; immaturity

Enlargement of Loop:

5. invest in the
lives of others

1. assess weaknesses, inadequa[cies]

2. confess sins, failures

4. appropriate
God's resources

I. SPIRITUAL
BIRTH
(beginning)

3. affirm self, others, God

natural course. There is no great opportunity for creativity or individuality in this stage, but, conversely, there is little danger of major conflict.

Sooner or later, however, we begin to question and challenge some of our teachings, and in doing so approach the second stage of growth in spiritual living. We are striving to ascertain the reason for the hope that [we] have within" (I Peter 3:15, Phillips). We are entering the "not quite" stage, where we are not quite a child, not quite an adult, and not quite sure. We experience a certain amount of negativism, perhaps even rebellion; at least we become vaguely discontented with the spiritual status quo. "There must be more to Christianity than this," we reason. Our Christian living is too ordinary; our God is too small. Great saints of the past and present have seemingly attained such heights in Christian living that we appear as midgets in comparison with them. Entering this stage we become aware of the tremendous opportunity for creativity, as well as the sense of conflict that interferes with that potential creativity.

Such an awareness produces a crisis: something must be done. In reconciling this conflict, there are several possibilities. Perhaps the most obvious option is *regression*: we may return to conventionality, group conformity and an earlier security, settling for a narrow "brand of Christianity" that lets others do our thinking and map out our spiritual lives for us.

A second possibility is *re-enslavement*: we allow the conflict and disillusionment to overcome and defeat us; we follow after other gods and fail to keep Christ in first place, and drift back into our former mode of living. A modification of this possibility is striking back rebelliously at God; we "cop out"; we react to our sense of frustration and seeming inability to work out our salvation by resorting to alcohol, drugs, LSD, or some other violent form of escapism.

A third alternative is *fixation*: we continue in rebellion and turmoil; our "religious life" is a joyless commitment in which we are rebellious, fault-finding, doubting and unloving. The Israelites, we will recall, wandered forty years in the wilderness before accepting God's leadings into the Promised Land.

A fourth path is *neurosis*: as "spiritual hypochondriacs" we develop an abnormal overconcern for our own spiritual welfare; we are absorbed in the task of feeling our spiritual pulse constantly; we carry with us fears and anxieties that put a severe "crimp" in our spiritual style.

A fifth possibility is *fanaticism*: we "split" off into a "spiritual psychosis" and become obsessed with "majoring in minors"; we are tossed to and fro with every wind of doctrine (Ephesians 4:14), and lose vital contact with the Lifegiver. We have a form of religion, but it lacks reality, depth and power.

There is, however, another alternative, and that is *surrender*. We embrace the way of faith, commitment and abandonment; the Holy Spirit takes control. We appropriate the power that has motivated the great souls of all ages, enabling them to overcome their self-centeredness and unholy fear. Thus all of our human faculties are reinforced and our personalities are unified.[180] This is the life, we confidently assert, that Christ has promised in John 10:10, "I came that they may have life, and have it abundantly."

We must note, however, that such a life is not easily attained. To reach the road marked "spiritual maturity" is to pass through much tension and conflict. The temptation to take other, more frequently traveled roads, is ever before us. But again, as in conversion, we reach the crisis point of rejecting all other roads and, in faith and obedience, trusting Christ to lead us along the road toward maturity.

Once on this road we find continuing tension and frustration and frequently are tempted to forsake the road for one seemingly less arduous. The "loops" are drawn in the model (see page 144) to show that the realistic day-to-day living is all too often composed of at least momentary hang-ups: sins, glaring imperfections, moods, destructive tensions, and an ever-present proneness to wander from the path of faith

---

[180]Jones, *The Way to Power and Poise*, p. 27.

and obedience. We are very much aware of our frailties and tendency to fail. But we refuse to allow ourselves to focus on our own weaknesses, or upon circumstances. Instead, we focus upon Christ: whole-heartedly affirming our relationship with Him, and appropriating and investing the exhaustless resources that He has placed at our disposal. And, in so doing, we find that the "path of the just is as the shining light, that shineth more and more unto the perfect day" (Proverbs 4:18, KJV).

Discussion Questions

1. Which contributor of ideas in Chapter 4 has the most to contribute to a sound philosophy of mental health? Why?

2. Is St. Augustine's idea sound: "Love God and do what you will"?

3. Is self-transcendence a more worthy goal than self-actualization? Why or why not?

4. For Rogers the good life involves, in part, a moving away from the "I-have-to-be-good" obsession and away from the compulsion to meet the expectations of society. Do you agree?

5. Do we over-simplify too much by maintaining that the highest spiritual and psychological wholeness comes about by affirming, appropriating and investing our resources received by belonging to Christ?

6. Is the developmental model of Christian growth with its loops a realistic view of your Christian experience?

7. What insights or benefits have you derived from reading this book?

Bibliography

Some books quoted with American Publishers may well be published also in Great Britain, and *vice versa*.

Adler, Alfred. *The Science of Living*. New York: Garden City Publishing Company, 1929.

Adler, Alred. *Understanding Human Nature*. Translated by Walter Béran Wolfe. New York: Greenburg, 1927.

Adler, Alfred. *What Life Should Mean to You*. New York: Capricorn Books, 1958.

Allport, Gordon W. *Becoming: Basic Considerations for a Psychology of Personality*. New Haven: Yale University Press, 1955.

Allport, Gordon W. *Personality: A Psychological Interpretation*. New York: Henry Holt and Company, 1937.

Allport, Gordon W. *The Individual and His Religion*. New York: The Macmillan Company, 1950.

Ames, Edward Scribner. "Religion and Childhood". *Readings in the Psychology of Religion*. Orlo Strunk, Jr. New York: Abingdon Press, 1959.

Ansbacher, Heinz L., and Rowena R. *The Individual Psychology of Alfred Adler*. A Basic Book. New York: Basic Books, 1956.

Arnold, Magda A., and Gasson, John A. *The Human Person*. New York: Ronald Press, 1954.

Berne, Eric. *Games People Play*. New York: Grove Press, 1964.

Boggs, Wade H., Jr. *All Ye Who Labor*. Richmond: John Knox Press, 1961.

Carnegie, Dale. *How to Stop Worrying and Start Living*. New York: Simon and Schuster, 1948.

Clark, Gordon H. *A Christian Philosophy of Education*. Grand Rapids: Eerdmans, 1946.

Cox, Harvey. *The Secular City*. New York: The Macmillan Company, 1965.

Cross, Hildreth. *An Introduction to Psychology*. Grand Rapids: Zondervan Publishing House, 1952.

Ehrenwald, Jan. *From Medicine Man to Freud.* A Dell Book. New York: Dell, 1956.

Fischer, Louis. "Gandhi's 'Soul Force' ". *Morality and Mental Health.* Edited by Hobart Mowrer. Chicago: Rand McNally and Company, 1967.

Fordham, Freida. *An Introduction to Jung's Psychology.* A Pelican Original. Baltimore: Penguin Books, 1953.

Fosdick, Harry Emerson. *On Being a Real Person.* A Harper Chapelbook. New York: Harper and Row, 1943.

Frankl, Viktor E. *Man's Search for Meaning.* Translated by Ibse Lasch. Revised ed. Boston: Beacon Press, 1962.

Frankl, Viktor E. *The Doctor and the Soul.* Translated by Richard and Clara Winston. 2nd ed. New York: Alfred A. Knopf, 1966.

Freeman, Lucy. *Why People Act That Way.* New York: Thomas Crowell, 1965.

Freeman, Lucy, and Small, Marvin. *The Story of Psychoanalysis.* A Pocket Book. New York: Pocket Books, 1960.

Freud, Sigmund. *Civilization and its Discontents.* Translated by Joan Riviere. London: The Hogarth Press, Limited, 1951.

Freud, Sigmund. *New Introductory Lectures on Psycho-Analysis.* Translated by W. J. H. Sprott. New York: W. W. Norton and Company, 1933.

Freud, Sigmund. "The Ego and the Id". *A General Selection from the Works of Sigmund Freud.* Edited by John Rickman. New York: Liveright Publishing Corporation, 1957.

Freud, Sigmund. *Totem and Taboo.* Translated by James Strachey. New York: W. W. Norton and Company, 1950.

Fromm, Erich. *Beyond the 'Chains of Illusion.* New York: Simon and Schuster, 1962.

Fromm, Erich. *Escape From Freedom.* New York: Holt, Rinehart and Winston, 1941.

Fromm, Erich. *Man for Himself.* New York: Rinehart and Company, 1947.

Fromm, Erich. *Psychoanalysis and Religion.* New Haven: Yale University Press, 1950.

Fromm, Erich. *The Art of Loving.* A Bantam Sixty. New York: Bantam Books, 1956.

Fromm, Erich. *The Sane Society.* New York: Rinehart and Company, 1955.

Gaede, Erwin A. "The Priesthood of Sinners". *Morality and Mental Health.* Edited by O. Hobart Mowrer. Chicago: Rand McNally and Company, 1967.

Hall, Calvin S., and Lindzey, Gardner. *Theories of Personality.* New York: John Wiley and Sons, 1957.

Henderson, Stella Van Petten. *Introduction to Philosophy of Education.* Chicago: The University of Chicago Press, 1947.

Hilgard, Ernest, and Atkinson, Richard C. *Introduction to Psychology.* 4th ed. New York: Harcourt, Brace and World, 1967.

Horney, Karen. *Neurosis and Human Growth.* New York: W. W. Norton and Company, 1950.

Horney, Karen. *New Ways in Psychoanalysis.* New York: W. W. Norton and Company, 1939.

Horney, Karen. *Our Inner Conflicts.* New York: W. W. Norton and Company, 1945.

Hostie, Raymond. *Religion and the Psychology of Jung.* Translated by G. R. Lamb. New York: Sheed and Ward, 1957.

Jacobi, Jolan. *The Psychology of Jung.* Translated by K. W. Bash. New Haven: Yale University Press, 1943.

James, William. *The Varieties of Religious Experience.* London: Longmans, Green and Company, 1911.

Jones, E. Stanley. *The Way to Power and Poise.* New York: Abingdon Press, 1949.

Jourard, Sidney. *The Transparent Self.* An Insight Book. Princeton: D. Van Nostrand Company, 1964.

Jung, Carl G. *Modern Man in Search of a Soul.* Translated by W. S. Dell, and Cary F. Baynes, New York: Harcourt, Brace and Company, 1933.

Jung, Carl G. *Psychology and Religion.* New Haven: Yale University Press, 1938.

Jung, Carl G. *The Undiscovered Self.* Translated by R. F. C. Hull. Boston: Little Brown and Company, 1957.

Karpf, Fay B. *The Psychology and Psychotherapy of Otto Rank.* New York: Philosophical Library, 1953.

Kazantzakis, Nikos. *Zorba the Greek.* Translated by Carl Wildman. New York: Simon and Schuster, 1953.

Kierkegaard, Soren. "Fear and Trembling". *The Sickness unto Death.* Translated by W. Lowrie. Anchor Books. New York: Doubleday and Company, 1968.

Kunkel, Fritz. *In Search of Maturity.* New York: Charles Scribners Sons, 1949.

Larson, Bruce. *Dare to Live Now!* Zondervan Books. Grand Rapids: Zondervan Publishing House, 1965.

Liebman, Joshua Loth. *Peace of Mind.* New York: Simon and Schuster, 1946.

Magill, Frank N., ed. *Masterpieces of World Philosophy in Summary Form.* New York: Harper and Brothers, 1961.

Maltz, Maxwell. *Psycho-Cybernetics*. A Wilshire Book. Hollywood: Wilshire Book Company, 1960.

Marx, Melvin H., and Hillix, William A. *Systems and Theories in Psychology*. New York: McGraw-Hill Book Company, 1963.

Maslow, Abraham H. *Motivation and Personality*. New York: Harper and Brothers, 1954.

Maslow, Abraham H. "Some Basic Propositions of A Growth and Self-Actualization Psychology". *Perceiving, Behaving, Becoming: A New Focus for Education*. 1962 Yearbook of the Association for Supervision and Curriculum Development. Washington: Association for Supervision and Curriculum Development, 1962.

Maslow, Abraham H. *Toward a Psychology of Being*. An Insight Book. Princeton: D. Van Nostrand Company, 1962.

Mavis, W. Curry. *The Psychology of Christian Experience*. Grand Rapids: Zondervan Publishing House, 1963.

May, Rollo, ed. *Existential Psychology*. New York: Random House, 1961.

May, Rollo. *Man's Search for Himself*. A Signet Book. New York: The New American Library, 1953.

May, Rollo. *Psychology and the Human Dilemma*. Princeton, New Jersey: D. VanNostrand Company, 1967.

May, Rollo. *The Art of Counseling*. Apex Books. New York: Abingdon Press, 1939.

May, Rollo. *The Meaning of Anxiety*. New York: The Ronald Press, 1950.

May, Rollo; Angel, Ernest; and Ellenberger, Henri F., eds. *Existence: A New Dimension in Psychiatry and Psychology*. A Clarion Book. New York: Simon and Schuster, 1958.

Mowrer, O. Hobart, ed. *Morality and Mental Health*. Chicago: Rand McNally and Company, 1967.

Mowrer, O. Hobart. *The Crisis in Psychiatry and Religion*. An Insight Book. Princeton, New Jersey: D. VanNostrand Company, 1961.

Mowrer, O. Hobart. *The New Group Therapy*. An Insight Book. Princeton, New Jersey: D. VanNostrand Company, 1964.

Murray, Henry A., *et al*. *Explorations in Personality*. New York: Oxford University Press, 1938.

Overstreet, Harry A. *The Mature Mind*. New York: W. W. Norton and Company, 1949.

Peale, Norman Vincent. *A Guide to Confident Living*. New York: Prentice-Hall, 1948.

Progoff, Ira. *The Death and Rebirth of Psychology*. New York: The Julian Press, 1956.

Rank, Otto. *Beyond Psychology*. New York: Dover Publications, 1958.

Rank, Otto. *Psychology and the Soul*. Translated by William D. Turner. Philadelphia: University of Pennsylvania Press, 1950.

Rank, Otto. *Will Therapy and Truth and Reality*. Translated by Jessie Taft. New York: Alfred A. Knopf, 1964.

Rees, Paul S. *The Adequate Man*. Westwood, New Jersey: Fleming H. Revell Company, 1959.

Riesman, David; Glazer, Nathan; and Denney, Reuel. *The Lonely Crowd: A Study of the Changing American Character*. New York: Doubleday and Company, 1953.

Rogers, Carl R. *On Becoming a Person*. Boston: Houghton Mifflin Company, 1951.

Rogers, Carl. "Two Divergent Trends". *Existential Psychology*. Edited by Rollo May. New York: Random House, 1960.

Ruch, Floyd L. *Psychology and Life*. 7th ed. Chicago: Scott, Foresman and Company, 1963.

Rushdoony, Rousas J. *Freud*. Modern Thinkers Series. Philadelphia: Presbyterian and Reformed Publishing Company, 1965.

Sheen, Fulton J. "Morbidity and the Denial of Guilt". *Morality and Mental Health*. Edited by O. Hobart Mowrer. Chicago: Rand McNally and Company, 1967.

Strunk, Orlo, Jr. Readings in the Psychology of Religion. New York: Abingdon Press, 1959.

Tallent, Norman. *Psychological Perspectives on the Person*. Insight Series. Princeton: D. VanNostrand Company, 1967.

Thomas, W. I. *The Unadjusted Girl*. Boston: Little, Brown, 1923.

Tournier, Paul. *Guilt and Grace*. Translated by Arthur W. Heathcote, J. J. Henry and P. J. Allcock. New York: Harper and Row, 1962.

Tournier, Paul. The Meaning of Persons. New York: Harper and Brothers, 1957.

Tweedie, Donald F., Jr. *Logotherapy and the Christian Faith*. Grand Rapids: Baker Book House, 1965.

Tweedie, Donald F., Jr. *The Christian and the Couch*. Grand Rapids: Baker Book House, 1963.

Weatherhead, Leslie D. *Psychology, Religion and Healing*. New York: Abingdon-Cokesbury Press, 1951.

Winn, Ralph B. *A Concise Dictionary of Existentialism*. New York: Philosophical Library, 1960.

PERIODICALS AND ENCYCLOPEDIAS

Carrel, Alexis. "Prayer is Power." *The Readers' Digest*, March 1941, pp. 34-36.

deBeauvoir, Simone. "An Existentialist Looks at Americans." *New York Times Magazine*, May 25, 1947, pp. 13, 51-54.

Grounds, Vernon. "Has Freud Anything for Christians?" *Eternity*, VII (July, 1956), p. 46.

Peale, Norman Vincent. "Picture It." *Guideposts*, May, 1967, pp. 22-23.

Schwartz, Morris S., and Charlotte G. "Mental Health: The Concept." *International Encyclopedia of the Social Sciences*. Vol. X.

Weisskopf-Joelson, Edith. "Some Comments on a Viennese School of Psychiatry." *Journal of Abnormal and Social Psychology*. 51 (1955), 701-03.

Acknowledgments

I wish to thank the following authors and publishers for permission to quote from copyrighted works:

Alexis Carrel, "Prayer is Power." *The Reader's Digest*, March, 1941.

Sigmund Freud, *Totem and Taboo*, trans. by James Strachey. W. W. Norton Co., New York, 1950.

Erich Fromm, *Psychoanalysis and Religion*. Yale University Press, New Haven, 1950.

Carl G. Jung, *Modern Man in Search of a Soul*, trans. by W. S. Dell and Cary F. Baynes. Harcourt, Brace and Co., New York, 1933.

Nikos Kazantzakis, *Zorba the Greek*, trans. by Carl Wildman. Simon and Schuster, 1953.

Abraham H. Maslow, "Some Basic Propositions of a Growth and Self-Actualization Psychology," in *Perceiving, Behaving, Becoming: A New Focus for Education*, 1962 Yearbook, Association for Supervision and Curriculum Development. Association for Supervision and Curriculum Development, Washington, 1962.

J. B. Phillips, *The New Testament in Modern English*. The Macmillan Company, 1958.

Otto Rank, *Will Therapy and Truth and Reality*, trans. by Jessie Taft. Alfred A. Knopf, New York, 1964.

Carl Rogers, *On Becoming a Person*. Houghton Mifflin Company, 1951.

Paul Tournier, *Guilt and Grace*, trans. by Arthur W. Heathcote, J. J. Henry and P. J. Allcock. Harper and Row, New York, 1962.

I wish also to express appreciation to three persons, without whose assistance this book never would have been written:

to Dr. David L. McKenna, who inspired the writer with the basic idea for the book,

to Mrs. Sandra Campbell, who carried the burden for the typing and proofreading of the book,

to Mr. Al Bryant, editor in chief of Zondervan Publishing House, whose comments, corrections and encouragement helped bring the project to its completion.

Index

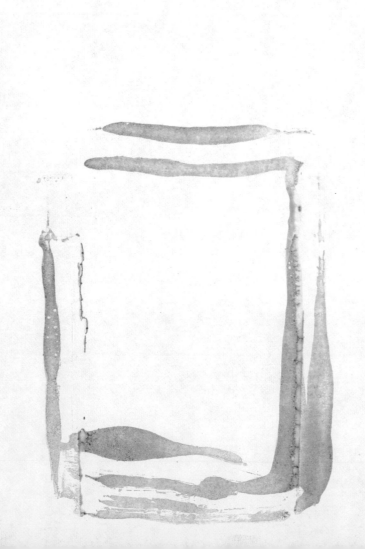